Jump-Start Your

CONFIDENCE

& Boost Your Self-Esteem

Jump-Start Your

CONFIDENCE

& Boost Your Self-Esteem

A Guide for Teen Girls: Unleash Your Inner Superpowers to
Destroy Fear and Self-Doubt, and Build
Unshakable Confidence

Book 3 of 3 from the
Words of Wisdom for Teens Series

Jacqui Letran

DUNEDIN, FLORIDA

Names: Letran, Jacqui.
Title: Jump Start Your Confidence & Boost Your Self-Esteem: A Guide for Teen Girls: Unleash Your Inner Superpowers to Destroy Fear and Self-Doubt and Build Unshakable Confidence / Jacqui Letran.
Description: 1st edition. | Dunedin, Florida: A Healed Mind, [2020] | Series: Words of Wisdom for Teens series; book 3 | Interest age level: 12 and up.
Identifiers: ISBN 978-1-952719-09-7 (hardcover) ISBN 978-1-952719-11-0 (paperback)
Subjects: LCSH: Adolescent psychology. | Teenagers--Attitudes. | Happiness in adolescence. | Emotions in adolescence. | Self-help techniques for teenagers.

Contents

Introduction

Do you often feel as though other people are better than you? Does it seem they are more carefree, more outgoing, and more confident? They make friends easily and good things seem to happen for them all the time. They are fun, witty, and full of charm. Everywhere they go, people are drawn to them. They do what they want and say what they think.

These positive, likable traits seem to come so naturally for them. But for you, life is filled with anxiety, fear, and self-doubt.

What is their secret? How can they talk to anyone about anything with ease, while it's a significant struggle for you to just be in the presence of others, let alone carry on a conversation?

You dream of being different. You dream of being comfortable in your own skin. You dream of creating meaningful relationships, going after what you want with confidence, and feeling happy and satisfied with your everyday life. But your fear and self-doubt may be holding you back, causing you to feel trapped and powerless to change your situation. You're left feeling sad, lonely, and insecure about yourself and your life.

What if there was a way to change all of that? What if you could destroy your fear and self-doubt and be strong and self-assured instead? What would it be like if you could go into any situation with excitement, courage, and confidence? Imagine what your life would look like and what you could achieve.

Just imagine.

I will let you in on a little secret. That excitement, courage, and confidence which you admire in others are skills that you can learn.

Sure, there are some people for whom these traits come naturally, but if you were not born with these traits, you can learn them. The thing is, you can learn to change your negative thinking, destroy your fear and self-doubt, and go after whatever you want with confidence. You can learn to be comfortable in your own skin and be completely at ease while expressing yourself.

You were born with incredible powers within yourself – powers I like to refer to as, Inner Superpowers (ISPs). When tapped into, these ISPs will help you be happy, resilient, and successful in life. The problem is that you have not been aware of these ISPs, nor how to use them.

Maybe you saw a glimpse of them here and there, but you didn't recognize their power or have faith in them. If you don't know what your ISPs are, how can you tap into them consistently and achieve the results you want and deserve?

In this book, you will learn:
- The seven Inner Superpowers guaranteed to destroy your fear and self-doubt

- Create a strong sense of self-esteem and unshakable confidence
- Easy to use tools to change your negative thinking into empowering thoughts
- How to connect to and strengthen your Inner Superpowers
- How to tap into and unleash your Inner Superpowers whenever you want to
- How to live within your full power and be happy, confident, and successful in life—and so much more!

You have so many Inner Superpowers that make you wonderful in every way. In this book, I have chosen to share seven specific ISPs because these seven are your best bet for destroying fear and self-doubt and for creating lasting self-esteem and unshakable confidence.

There is much written about each of these ISPs and each ISPs can be a stand-alone book. However, I know your time is valuable and you have other responsibilities and activities to tend to. Therefore, you'll find that these chapters are brief and to the point.

I will present enough information for you to understand your ISPs without bogging you down with too much information. By reading this book and completing the activities within each section, you will learn how to tap into these ISPs consistently, harness them, and unleash them whenever you want. You can learn how to go after what you want with confidence and create that happy and successful life you've been dreaming about.

NOTE: To get the most benefit from this book, work on each Inner Superpower in the order presented, as the concepts of each build to the next.

CHAPTER 1

It's All in Your Mind

Your mind has everything to do with your Inner Superpowers. It is essential for you to understand how your mind works so you can truly tap into it and change your negative thinking into positive, and powerful thoughts.

In this book, I will give you an overview of the inner workings of your mind. If you would like to go deeper into this topic, you can reread the second book in this series, entitled *I would, but MY DAMN MIND won't let me*, where this topic is discussed in depth.

Your Conscious and Subconscious Mind

Your conscious mind is your logical mind. It's the part of your mind that you are aware of. It's the part of your mind that you use when you focus on things or learn new things.

For example, your conscious mind helps you to learn how to play a sport, such as tennis. When you are in the learning phase, you consciously focus on learning proper techniques, such as how to hold the racquet properly, how to position your body to prepare for the incoming ball, and the proper way to move your body to create an effective swing. These thoughts and actions are the work of your conscious mind—something you are aware of and actively focusing on.

Your conscious mind is also responsible for helping you make decisions based on the things in front of you and the things you've learned from previous experiences. It is the part of your mind that makes simple decisions such as, "I want to wear shorts today because it's a warm day."

It also makes more complex decisions such as, "Should I lie to my mom so I can get out of trouble, but risk having her find out and getting even more upset with me?"

Your conscious mind does not work fully until around seven years old. This is why you believed in the Tooth Fairy, the Easter Bunny, and Santa Claus (not to mention your imaginary best friend) when you were a little kid. Before seven, you don't have a fully working logical mind that says, "That's not true because I've learned so-and-so and that doesn't match what I've learned."

As you get older and your conscious mind develops more and more, you begin to question whether those beliefs are true. Eventually, you stop believing in the Tooth Fairy, the Easter Bunny, and Santa Claus because your conscious mind is fully formed, and you can logically decide based on the facts you have learned over the years.

Your subconscious mind differs greatly from your conscious mind. The first important difference is that you are not aware of, nor can you control, what happens in your subconscious mind. Everything that happens in the subconscious part of your mind is happening without you knowing and without your control. In fact, everything that happens in your subconscious mind happens automatically, as if it's a program running on autopilot in the background.

Your subconscious mind works immediately at birth and one of its biggest jobs is to keep you alive and safe. However, to the subconscious mind, "safe" doesn't mean "safe" the way you probably define it today. Instead, "safe" means "Do not change. Stay exactly the way you are. Change is scary. Change is dangerous. If you try to change, you will get hurt."

When you are doing something new or outside of your belief system, your subconscious mind freaks out. It believes that you are putting yourself at risk for failure, rejection, or pain. So, it will do whatever it can to get you back to your "safe" place, which means going back to your old ways and staying exactly how you are right now.

To get you back to your "safe" place, your subconscious mind uses fear tactics to prevent you from taking actions and moving forward. It will do whatever it needs to do to get you to stop doing that new activity and return you to where you were. This is why a lot of people report feeling "stuck" when they are dealing with unhappy or difficult situations.

How many times have you wanted to do something, especially something new and a little scary, and immediately started feeling anxious and full of self-doubt? Even though you really wanted to do that thing, all you could think of is how you could end up failing, hurting, or embarrassing yourself. Instead of following through and doing what you wanted to do, you stop and retreat to your familiar pattern.

That's your subconscious mind at work. Your subconscious mind knows when you are fearful or anxious, chances are you'll stop what you're thinking about doing or attempting to do and go back to your old ways, the "safe" and familiar ways. Every time you attempt something and retreat, you reinforce your beliefs of "I can't" or "This is who I am."

Your Subconscious Mind Simplified

Let's explore your subconscious mind a little more; once you understand how your subconscious mind works, it will be so much easier to access your Inner Superpowers.

First, I want you to think of your subconscious mind as a collection of movies within a movie library. In this movie library, there are hundreds of thousands of movies—all starring YOU! Imagine there's a DVD for everything you have ever thought, felt, or done. That's a lot of DVDs, isn't it?

In your movie library is your personal assistant, which is really your subconscious mind. Its job is to continue to record your movies, store them, and replay them at the right time for you. In addition, your subconscious mind has a bigger job: to keep you safe. Unfortunately, more often than not, that means creating anxiety, fear, and self-doubt to prevent you from moving into the perceived unsafe territory.

Also, your subconscious mind is programmed to give you whatever experience you're looking for in the easiest, quickest way possible. Yes, you read that right! Your subconscious mind is programmed to give you whatever experience you're looking for, in the easiest, quickest way possible—as long as the thing you want matches your belief system. How you have perceived all of your experiences so far has been because of the requests you have made to your subconscious mind.

You might think, "But I didn't ask for all the stress or pain that I'm experiencing, nor for all those judgments I've been receiving."

While it might not seem like you've asked for those experiences, you did. You didn't know that you were asking for them because you don't fully understand how your mind works, or the enormous potential of your Inner Superpowers yet. (Hint: They are the key to radically changing how you ask for future experiences!).

Let me explain how you've been asking your mind for your experiences so far. Every single thought and feeling you have is a direct command to your subconscious mind, "This is the experience I want to have. Give me this experience."

Therefore, when you were getting ready for that presentation in class and you imagined how nervous you will be when it's your turn, you gave your subconscious mind these commands, "I want to be nervous during the presentation. This is the experience that I want. Give me this experience. Make sure I'm nervous during the presentation."

Being a loyal and faithful assistant, your subconscious mind goes to work immediately and scans your environment, searching for anything that could cause you to be nervous. The moment it finds something that could cause you to feel nervous, it directs all your attention to that thing.

At the same time, your subconscious mind will look into your movie library, looking for past movies that could cause you to feel nervous about your current situation. It will replay those movies for you automatically in the background of your mind. In addition, it creates a new movie of what could happen in your future based on your past experiences and the current experience you're asking for.

Not only does your subconscious replay all the times you were nervous presenting in front of the class, but it also starts playing the new movie it just made of you stumbling on your words and failing miserably during your presentation today. By the time it's your turn to present, you have become so nervous that all you can focus on is the sweatiness of your palms, the shakiness of your voice, and all those judgmental looks from your classmates.

The good news is that once you understand your subconscious mind and your Inner Superpowers, you can purposefully send the right commands to your subconscious mind in a positive and powerful way. That way, your subconscious mind can bring you a much better experience than what you have been through in the past.

A moment ago, I mentioned that your subconscious mind's job is to give you the experience you're looking for as long as it matches your current belief system. Your belief system is the program of your subconscious mind that runs on autopilot in the background. Whatever you believe is true is what your subconscious mind will continuously look for evidence of.

Similar to the concept that all thoughts and feelings are direct commands to your subconscious mind ("This is the experience I want; give me this experience."), your belief systems are also direct commands. However, belief systems are more powerful because they run automatically in the back of your mind all day. You don't even have to request these experiences actively through your thoughts and feelings.

As humans, we have this need to be right and our subconscious mind will work hard to make sure that this need is fulfilled. To complete this task, your subconscious mind will generalize, distort, or delete details so that the only experiences you have will match your belief system.

For example, if you have a belief that you are forgetful, your subconscious mind will ignore each instance of you remembering details or will distort it and call it "pure luck" or "a coincidence" when you catch yourself remembering something. You remember so much more than you forget, but when you forget something, your subconscious mind will happily bring it to your awareness.

Another example of how your subconscious mind will make sure your experiences match your beliefs is through generalization. Let's say a dog bit you when you were young, and that experience caused you significant pain and fear. To protect you from another similar painful episode, your mind might create the generalization that "all dogs are mean and will bite you." This causes you to hate dogs and you feel fearful whenever you're around any dog.

Unfortunately, dogs are great at picking up on when someone doesn't like them or when someone is fearful of them. To protect themselves, dogs will act aggressively when you are nearby because they sense your dislike and fear. This generalization allows you to be right and even influences the world around you (a dog in this case) to provide you with the experience that "all dogs are mean," when in fact, most dogs are rather sweet.

Commanding Your Subconscious Mind

A moment ago, you learned that every thought you have and every feeling you feel is a command to your subconscious mind to give you more of the same experience.

Here are three more important details for you to command your mind effectively.

Negative Commands Confuse Your Mind

Your subconscious mind does not know how to process negative commands. Negative commands are commands such as, "I don't want" or "I'm no longer" or "I'm not." Basically, they are any command that focuses on what you are *not*, or what you *don't* want. This is because for your subconscious mind to fully understand your command, it has to create a picture or to clearly "see" the experience you're looking for.

Let's say you wanted your brother to bring you your blue sweater, and you said to him, "Can you go to my room and bring me my sweater? I don't want the orange one." What are the chances that your brother would know you want him to bring you the *blue* sweater? Pretty slim—unless you only have two sweaters, an orange one and a blue one. Even then, wouldn't it be better to say to him, "Bring me the blue sweater," so he knows what color to look for and can find it quickly for you?

Your subconscious mind works the same way. When you give the command, "I don't want to be sad," it might seem like a good command at first because you don't want to be sad. But that command doesn't help your mind understand your true request. All it knows is that you don't want the experience of being sad, but it does not understand what experience you want instead. Your subconscious mind doesn't know if you want to feel angry, overwhelmed, unmotivated, disgusted, or many other feelings.

To help your subconscious mind understand your command, it creates a picture for each of the words in the command that can have an associated image, which are "I" and "sad" in this example. The mental picture of this command is, therefore, an image of you being sad. Then, the command becomes, "I want to be sad."

It is so important to focus on what you want rather than what you don't want. If you gave the command, "I want to be happy," or "I want to be relaxed," your subconscious mind would understand it and could bring that to you easily.

Weak Versus Strong Commands

Your commands could be viewed as strong or weak commands. Strong commands get your subconscious mind's attention immediately and direct your subconscious mind effectively.

One way to think about this is by knowing that you are the boss of your mind. As a boss, you can be firm or weak with your commands. To command your subconscious mind effectively and get your desired results, choose strong, powerful commands. Commands such as, "I choose," "I'm ready," "I'm determined," or "I'm committed to," are very strong commands.

Think about it. When you say, "I am determined to be an A student," how does that look in your mind's eye? How does that feel?

Now, try for the same outcome, but with a weaker command. "I hope I'll be an A student." How is this picture different in your mind? How does this command make you feel?

In the "determined" picture, you are in charge of your outcome. Chances are you'll see yourself confidently going after what you want to achieve. You might see yourself putting energy and effort into studying. You might see yourself pushing through barriers to achieve success.

In the "hope" picture, you might see yourself as uncertain as you attempt to work toward your goal. The energy and effort you're putting into those activities are not as strong or as persistent as your "determined" picture. Sure, you may do some work, but you'll leave more to chance.

Weak commands to avoid are commands such as "I wish," "I want," or "I hope." When you wish, want, or hope for a result, your attitude about how to proceed isn't as solid or as powerful as when you are ready, determined, or committed to your goal.

Vague Comparative Commands Don't Help

Your subconscious mind is very literal, which could cause it to believe that it has successfully given you the experiences you've asked for when, in fact, it hasn't When you give your subconscious mind a Vague Comparative Command that sounds like, "I wish I had more money," the "more money" part of that sentence is a comparison of one thing to another. Yet, it doesn't really identify what it's being compared to.

What does "more money" mean, exactly? More money than you've had in your life? More money than whom? If you had one penny more than you did a minute ago, you do, in fact, have more money, but I doubt that's what your intention was when you made the request.

If you said, "I am determined to have $100 more than I have right now," your subconscious mind knows exactly what you want, doesn't it?

Suppose you give your subconscious mind the command, "I want to be happier." Again, happier than when? Happier than whom? To your subconscious mind, if you are happier now than you were last week (when you were overwhelmingly depressed), then it would believe that it has already successfully delivered the experience you're asking for and it doesn't have to do anything else other than to continue to give you the same experience.

Strong, powerful, and clear commands such as, "I am committed to being happy," or "I'm ready to be happy," are great alternatives. When you use these commands, your subconscious mind will get busy looking for reasons for you to be happy in that moment and evidence that you are committed to your happiness.

Remember, to give your subconscious mind the most powerful commands:

1. Focus on your desired outcome and be specific.
2. Stop focusing on the things you don't want or the condition you want to move away from.
3. Use strong command words such as "choose," "ready to," "committed to," and "determined to.
4. Avoid Vague Comparative Commands such as "more" or "better than." If you give a

comparative command, it is best to give a specific comparison.

Stop Watching Those Crappy Movies

Think of a type of movie that you absolutely hate to watch because it's uncomfortable, or it stresses you out. For me, it's gory, violent movies. For the sake of this example, let's pretend that you also hate to watch gory, violent movies.

Now, imagine you just had a very stressful day, and you want to relax and watch something on TV to take your mind off your stress. You sit down on your couch and turn on the television. In front of you is the goriest, most violent movie you have ever seen and the sound of people screaming in pain is blasting loudly. What would you do in that instance?

Chances are you would turn the TV off, change the channel, or go do something else. Would you ever sit in front of that television screen and think, "Please let this movie end. I can't stand this movie. I feel so helpless that this movie is playing in front of me. There is nothing I can do to stop this movie. I'm just a victim."

Of course, you wouldn't think these thoughts in this situation! That would be silly because you have the power to leave, turn the TV off, or change the channel. At that moment, you would take control and be the boss of that situation, wouldn't you?

What if I told you that you do, in fact, sit in front of unpleasant movies and act like a powerless victim quite often? Would it surprise you to know that you do this? Well, my dear reader, you do, in fact, do this a lot.

How often do you replay a scene of a real or perceived failure in your mind? What about recalling every single detail of an argument, or how someone once mistreated you? How many times have you replayed the movie where you embarrassed yourself in front of your friends or classmates? When you think about those events, how did you feel? Did you feel powerful and confident, or did you find yourself full of anxiety, fear, or self-doubt?

Remember earlier, when I said your subconscious mind is a room full of movies about you? Every time you replay an argument or beat yourself up for something that happened in the past, all you are doing is replaying that crappy movie, repeatedly, and watching it as if you are powerless to change the channel. You play some movies so many times they have found their way onto your automatic "favorite playlist."

You don't have to watch those movies or listen to the recording of them anymore. You can turn them off. Just like a television, you have different channels in your mind. If you have an experience you don't like, be willing to change the station to something else or turn the television off completely. I will show you how to do this when I teach you about your Inner Superpowers.

I hope by now, you are getting a lot of "Ah-Ha!" moments and things are making sense for you. Let's dive into those Inner Superpowers now, so you can start taking charge of yourself and your life.

Self-Reflection

Take five minutes to think about how your life will look once you understand your Inner Superpowers and can tap into them consistently to destroy your fear and self-doubt. What would that look like? What would you do next? How would your life be different?

Use your imagination and have fun with this self-reflection. Write down all the wonderful things you can do now because you are strong, confident, and courageous. Remember to dream big.

_____

_____

_____

_____

_____

_____

_____

_____

_____

_____

_____

_____

_____

_____

_____

_____

_____

_____

_____

_____

_____

_____

_____

_____

_____

_____

_____

_____

_____

_____

_____

_____

_____

_____

_____

_____

_____

_____

_____

CHAPTER 2

The Power of Words

Words are one of our greatest and most frequently used Inner Superpowers. Words can create significant insecurities, destroy relationships, and tear families apart. Words can also have an equally positive effect. It can give a hopeless person hope, heal a broken heart, and give someone the power and courage to pursue their dreams.

You might be thinking, "Wait a minute—aren't words external? How can they be an Inner Superpower?"

Great questions! Words are an Inner Superpower because your words come from within yourself. These include the words you speak out loud, but more importantly, also the words you say to yourself when you think and analyze situations.

Why Words Are a Superpower

Have you ever done something that you were really proud of and were really excited to share that achievement with your friends and family? However, the moment you shared your accomplishment with someone, you immediately feel deflated, embarrassed, or maybe even sad.

Perhaps the words they responded with made you feel criticized. Perhaps the words they used made you feel as though you're not good enough. You might start to doubt yourself or even call yourself names. You might wonder if you are lame or even stupid for being so proud of something that no one else seemed to care about.

You are not alone in this pattern of thinking and feeling. We all have had similar negative thoughts in the back of our minds at different times that caused us to feel sad, scared, uncomfortable, or full of self-doubt. How destructive is that way of thinking?

Just a moment ago, you were feeling great. But because someone said harsh or unsupportive words to you, your happiness level plummeted. Not only did your happiness level plummet, but perhaps your self-belief and self-confidence took a dive just as quickly. Often, you will start using negative words to yourself after these types of events. Maybe you think, "I'm a loser. No one cares about me or what I do."

Those silent conversations you have with yourself are exceptionally powerful because you may not even realize that they are happening. Even so, your subconscious mind is paying attention and is looking for evidence to fulfill your request to experience being a loser that no one cares about.

All of this works together to create significant negative emotions that result in you doubting yourself, your abilities, and maybe even your self-worth. That's the power of words. They can take you from total excitement and happiness to sadness, fear, and self-doubt in a flash.

The good news is that words can also have a powerfully positive effect. Imagine a time that you felt down, frustrated, isolated, and alone. Now, imagine that someone reached out to you and said just the right words—words you desperately wanted or needed to hear at that moment.

Perhaps you were feeling a lot of pain and uncertainty and a friend reached out to you and said, "You're going to be OK. I'm here for you." You went from feeling sad, alone, or frustrated to feeling a lot better almost immediately. Perhaps you might even feel safe, supported, loved, or happy. Because of these kind and supportive words, your mood changed; and it changed at the speed of thought!

You start seeing possibilities where there were only limitations before. Rather than retreating, you look for ways to move past this block. You feel motivated. You see solutions easily and you feel confident in your ability to solve your problems, or maybe you see a way out. This is the positive power of words!

Word Filters

Your words have immense powers. Whatever words you use to express your thoughts or feelings, whether out loud or silently to yourself, are the same words that create your reality and life experiences. In this way, it is very similar to editing a picture using a filter app.

Imagine taking a vibrant and colorful photo and putting a black and white filter on it. What would happen? Would your picture remain vibrant and colorful, or would it change into a black-and-white picture? If you are editing a photo using a particular filter and you don't like the result, are you going to say, "Oh, well. There's nothing I could do about it"? Or would you try out a different filter? Most likely, you would try a different filter or at least revert to the original picture.

Our life experiences are very similar to that. Just imagine your words are the filters, or "Word Filters," and your life experiences are the photos. Whatever Word Filters you choose to put on your life experiences will become the result you see in your "photos," which is your reality. When you have an experience you don't like, be willing to play around with different Word Filters and create the pictures you want at that moment.

For example, let's say you tried out for a lead role in your school play, and you were not chosen. The Word Filters that naturally pop up for you might sound like, "I don't deserve that part because I'm a terrible actor. Everyone else is so much better than me. Who am I kidding? I'm no good at this. Why do I even bother?"

When you use these Word Filters to view your experience, how do you feel? Do you feel positive and encouraged, or do you feel sad and deflated?

Instead of allowing your old Word Filters to control your mood, what if you decided to use your Inner Superpower of Words to express yourself? What if you choose to think or say, "That actor got the role because they have three more years of experience than I do. I am a beginner, and I am committed to learning and practicing so I can be my best," or "I am not the right person for this part and the right part for me will come along." When you use these Word Filters, how do you feel? Do you feel sad and deflated, or do you feel motivated to improve yourself and inspired to look for new opportunities?

The reality of the situation is that you did not get the lead role. However, how you choose to view that event will either lift you up and prepare you for the next opportunity or drag you down and discourage your ambitions. The choice is yours.

Your words are that powerful. And if you are careless with your words, you can create unwanted (and unnecessary!) pain and misery for yourself and others around you. Be purposeful in the words you use to create the experiences you want for yourself and those you care about. Choose words that are supportive, encouraging, and inspiring when you speak to yourself and others. You can create your experiences by selecting the words that empower you.

The Power of "I AM"

In the English language, the two most powerful words, when used together, are the words "I AM." Whatever you put behind "I AM" becomes your reality. The words that immediately follow "I AM" are your declaration to your subconscious mind and the Universe: "This is who I am. Make sure I have this experience."

Let's say you're going to a party and you're feeling a little nervous. You worry that you'll have a bad time because you believe people don't like you or that you are awkward and won't fit in. Imagine entering the party with these thoughts, "I AM going to be so uncomfortable. I AM so nervous. I AM going to feel and act so awkward."

These are your declarations and commands to your subconscious mind to make sure you have these experiences. Your subconscious mind will hear those thoughts as commands, "I want to have a bad time. Make sure I feel like I don't fit in. Make sure I feel so uncomfortable, nervous, and awkward."

Being that dedicated assistant, your subconscious mind will go to work and adjust your environment so that no matter where you look, you will get to experience the party through the Word Filters of your negative "I AM" commands.

As you sit in the corner by yourself, looking nervously around, you happen to lock eyes with someone who has an unpleasant expression on her face; maybe you see it as a disgusted expression.

Immediately, you start thinking, "I KNEW IT! I shouldn't be here. Everyone thinks I'm a weirdo. What was I thinking? I'm so stupid to think I could fit in or have fun." Look what has happened—a new flood of negative commands that will reinforce your experience and your beliefs!

How damaging are your words to your confidence and self-esteem? Because you glanced up and saw someone with an unpleasant expression on her face and the Word Filters you're using are negative ones, you instantly came to a destructive conclusion that caused you to feel worse about yourself and your situation.

In reality, perhaps that girl was thinking, "I got all dressed up for Tommy and he won't even look at me. He doesn't think I'm attractive." Or maybe she's thinking, "OMG, I forgot to turn the curling iron off at home. I'm going to burn the house down! I always do stupid things like this," and the disgusted look on her face reflects her fear and her own self-judgments, which has nothing to do with you at all.

These two examples show how we are all "in our own minds," thinking about our problems. The experiences we have are of our own creation based on the words we choose when we talk to ourselves. We are all guilty of creating these negative stories in our minds. We make ourselves fearful, sad, or anxious for no reason other than because we don't feel good about ourselves in those moments, and we are not fully aware of the power of our words.

How to Destroy Fear and Self-Doubt Using the Power of Words

If you feel nervous at any event or situation, you can take control by unleashing your Inner Superpower of Words and select a different set of Word Filters. Maybe you can choose a couple of these different Word Filters instead:

- "I AM OK. Everything will be OK."
- "I AM willing to have fun."
- "I AM calm."
- "I AM excited to try something new."
- "I AM courageous."
- "I AM excited to meet new people."
- "I AM ready to enjoy myself."

When you choose positive Word Filters like these, you give your subconscious mind an entirely different set of commands. You are telling your subconscious mind to use the lenses that allow you to have positive experiences. You might even find yourself having fun and connecting with people like never before because you have actively chosen to use your Inner Superpower of Words to create meaningful experiences for yourself.

Now that you are aware of the Inner Superpower of Words, I encourage you to go through the following exercises to help you master this power. With practice, you can easily and effectively destroy your fear and self-doubt.

Self-Reflection

Spend a few minutes answering these questions and coming up with examples for the following:

1. On a scale of 0 to 10 (with 10 being the highest), how aware was I of how my words impacted myself and others prior to reading this chapter? How aware am I now?

_____

_____

2. Here are two examples of how the words I have been using created pain for myself:

_____

_____

_____

_____

_____

_____

_____

_____

_____

_____

3. Here are two examples of how the words I have been using created pain for someone else:

_____

_____

_____

_____

_____

_____

_____

_____

_____

_____

_____

4. Here are two examples of how the words I have been using have supported, inspired, or motivated myself:

_____

_____

_____

_____

_____

_____

_____

_____

_____

_____

_____

_____

5. Here are two examples of how the words I have been using have supported, inspired, or motivated others:

_____

_____

_____

_____

_____

_____

_____

_____

_____

_____

_____

6. When I do something wrong, or when something doesn't go as planned, the words I often use when talking to myself are:

_____

_____

_____

_____

_____

_____

_____

_____

_____

_____

_____

7. Now that I understand the power of my words, I am ready to choose my words wisely. Here are a few empowering words or Word Filters I can choose instead:

Example:
- "I'm a beginner at ____ and that's OK."
- "Well, that didn't work out. Let's try_____ instead."
- "I know I can do better with practice."
- "I'm ready to dedicate time to achieving my goals."

Your turn: Create three to four Word Filters you can use in the future.

_____

_____

_____

_____

_____

_____

_____

_____

_____

_____

_____

_____

_____

_____

CHAPTER 3

The Power of Your Body

Your body is one of your most powerful Inner Superpowers. Your body is how you represent yourself (how you "show up" or appear) to the rest of the world.

Your body position, your facial expression, and how you move your body tells others so much about who you are. Even before people have a chance to get to know you, they will have already made a lot of assumptions about you based on your physical appearance and how you carry yourself.

When you understand the Inner Superpower of Your Body, you can show up as a warm and confident person who people are excited to meet and get to know. When I'm talking about the Inner Superpower of Your Body, I'm not talking about how you're dressed or the size of your clothes—although they could support you in feeling good about yourself. Your true power is in how you control your body.

How you move your body has the power to influence your moods dramatically. Therefore, it has a significant impact on your experiences. In the past, it was commonly believed that our minds were fully responsible for controlling our bodies, therefore our actions. In recent years, Embodied Cognition,[1] a newer field of cognitive science (the study of the mind), emerged to show that "the mind is not only connected to the body, but that the body influences the mind." What this means is that our minds influence our bodies, and our bodies influence our minds.

The findings within Embodied Cognition research are so exciting because it helps us to understand the very important roles our bodies play in influencing our moods, actions, and experiences. When you understand how simple these concepts are, you will be able to tap into the Inner Superpower of Your Body to quickly and instantly destroy your fear and self-doubt while boosting your confidence level.

In simple terms, your mind, or the thoughts and feelings you have, influences how your body reacts. Likewise, the actions and positions of your body influence how you feel, which, in turn, affects your thoughts, actions, and experiences.

Why Your Body is a Superpower

To fully understand the power of your body, let's talk about two very key concepts, the Mind's Programs and the Body's Programs.

The Mind's Programs
_____

[1] McNerney, Samuel. A Brief Guide to Embodied Cognition: Why You Are Not Your Brain "http://blogs.scientificamerican.com/guest-blog/a-brief-guide-to-embodied-cognition-why-you-are-not-your-brain/

Have you ever noticed that when you're feeling an intense emotion, such as sadness, everything around you, including the small things that you typically wouldn't even notice, can cause you to feel even worse?

This is because whenever you have a certain emotion, your subconscious mind will automatically run the corresponding "mind's program" for that emotion. A mind's program can be thought of the same way as a computer program, which is a set of procedures or commands for your mind to carry out. The purpose of these emotional mind's programs is to give you—and enhance—the experience you've asked for.

In a previous chapter, you learned that your thoughts and feelings are direct commands to your subconscious mind: "This is the experience I want. Give me this experience." When you are feeling sad, you're giving your subconscious mind the command of, "I want to feel sad. Give me this experience." Your subconscious mind will immediately run your mind's program for sadness.

With the Mind's Program for sadness running, your subconscious mind will look in your movie library and find movies from your past that caused you sadness and start playing those movies in a repetitive loop. This brings those past events back into your awareness, causing you to re-experience the pain from those events again.

You stay stuck in your head, thinking about all these different painful events and your sadness persists. Perhaps you're thinking about a certain mistake you've made repeatedly. Perhaps you're thinking about all the times people have rejected you and caused you pain. Or perhaps you're thinking about all the times you've let yourself or someone else down.

At the same time your old movies are playing in the background, your subconscious mind will scan your environment, looking for evidence for why you should be sad. Anything that has the potential of making you feel sad will be picked up by your subconscious mind and pointed out to you. You become hyperaware of the things that make you sad, while the things that could make you happy get completely ignored.

Each time you play your mind's program for sadness and experience sadness, your beliefs about sadness and who you are in relation to sadness become stronger. You feel trapped within this loop, which could make you feel as though you are powerless against these repetitive thoughts. These negative, reoccurring thoughts can even lead you down a path of greater sadness and create feelings of anxiety, hopelessness, or even depression.

As if that's not bad enough, your subconscious mind will take another step to enhance the experience you've requested. Using the evidence it has picked up on from your past movies, your subconscious mind will create a new movie for you. Only this time, it is set in the future. In this movie, you are still trapped in the repetitive patterns that caused your sadness—you're still letting yourself and others down and people are still rejecting and hurting you. This little gift from your subconscious mind helps to keep you in the experience you had asked for.

This is a very common path for the mind's program for most emotions. When you are in a particular emotional state, your subconscious mind will do everything it can to continue or heighten that feeling for you. It will replay your past movies, look for external evidence, and project similar events into your future. The net result is that you get to continue experiencing more of those same feelings.

Remember, you asked for the experience and your subconscious mind is just doing its job and being a good assistant to you.

The Body's Programs

Your body also has its own programs for your various emotions. To simplify, I will call them the "strong body program" and the "weak body program."

Typically, when you feel anxious, inferior, scared, or another similar negative emotion, your body will run the "weak body program." When the weak body program is running, you and your body tend to close up. Your shoulders might start feeling heavy or tight and your gaze might start going downward. You might start slouching, crossing your arms or legs, or even curling yourself up into the fetal position. When you feel bad about yourself or your situation, your body naturally becomes smaller, as if to hide or protect you from any real or perceived danger.

The opposite is true for when you are feeling self-assured, happy, or powerful and you are running the "strong body program." When you feel good about yourself, your body naturally opens up and your gaze is either focused ahead or upward.

A study[2] comparing blind Olympic athletes (some who were blind at birth) with athletes who can see normally shows how dramatically similar the athletes moved their bodies in response to winning or losing an

---

[2] Yong, Ed. Blind Olympic athletes show the universal nature of pride and shame. http://phenomena.nationalgeographic.com/2008/08/13/blind-olympic-athletes-show-the-universal-nature-of-pride-and-shame/

event. "The winners tilted their heads up, smiled, lifted their arms, clenched their fists and puffed out their chests, while slumped shoulders and narrowed chests were the hallmarks of losers."

Isn't that interesting? Even the athletes who were blind from birth and who have never witnessed another person's body movement would display the same body movements in response to winning or losing. This is because we are born with these automatic body programs for our feelings, and they are almost identical from person to person.

Think of a time when you aced a difficult test, scored the winning point for your team, or were chosen to participate in something you were really excited about. How did you react physically? Perhaps you gave your friends high-fives. Perhaps you jumped up and down or danced. Or perhaps you puffed out your chest and threw your hands up in the victory position. Every one of those actions demonstrates your body's program for positivity and success. When you feel good about yourself, your body naturally opens up and takes up more space as if to say, "Look at me!"

Similarly, think of a time when you did something that you were really embarrassed about or ashamed of. How did your body react? Did you make direct eye contact with those around you? Did you stand there with your hands on your hips and proudly display your embarrassment or shame, or did you slink away hoping to go unnoticed?

The Mind's and The Body's Program at Work

Let's go back to the mind's program for sadness to show how the mind's and body's programs work together. Once you've triggered the mind's program for an emotion, it runs on autopilot. Your body reacts accordingly by triggering the matching body's program.

Let's say you got into a fight with a friend and now, you're feeling sad. Your sad mind's program kicks in. You start to think about all the other times this friend has caused you pain. Your thoughts might shift to other people who have hurt you and other sad events from your past. You might even think about how this friend will hurt you again in the future.

At the same time, your body naturally responds by closing up. Your energy closes in; you cross your arms over your chest, curl yourself up in a little ball, or become listless. You might even feel mentally, emotionally, and physically drained. You don't want to do anything or talk to anyone. You just want to lie there, curled up in your misery.

All of this happens simultaneously because your mind and your body are working together, running their individual programs, to bring you the experience you've asked for, which, in this example, is sadness. Suddenly, you went from feeling a little sad to feeling very sad. If you do nothing about it and allow these programs to run, you will continue to stay sad.

Here's where it gets really exciting! Your mind and your body have to run the same program for you to continue to stay in your current emotional experience. This is really important, so let me say it again.

Your mind and your body have to run the
same program for your mind to continue

*its path and hang onto your current
emotional state.*

When your mind and your body are not running the same program, your mind gets confused. When your mind gets confused, it stops running the current emotional program and your feelings change. In this way, your body is very powerful in its ability to influence your feelings.

How to Destroy Fear and Self-Doubt Using the Power of Your Body

How can you use this information to boost your confidence and destroy your fear and self-doubt?

Let's say you're feeling anxious and your mind's program for anxiety is running and causing you to think and remember more anxiety-inducing events. Your body reacts accordingly and kicks in the body's program for anxiety. You notice your body starting to close in and that you have crossed your arms. You notice that you're looking down toward the ground and you're shifting uncomfortably where you're standing.

When you notice your body closing up, what if you decided to tap into your Inner Superpower of Your Body and do something different? Instead of allowing your body to close up, what if you decided to open it up? What if you stand tall and strong, throw your arms up, look up at the sky, and smile the biggest, most confident, or even goofy smile you can imagine? How do you think you would feel if you just changed your body like that?

Let's do a quick exercise to show you what this looks like. Start by standing up with your feet hip-width distance apart. Tighten up your leg muscles and feel how strong your legs are. Stand up tall and look straight ahead and smile the biggest smile you can. Also, either place your hands on your hips or throw them up toward the sky.

How do you feel when you hold your body this way? What happens to your self-confidence level?

For the sake of this activity, go ahead and do the opposite. Start slouching your body, allow your shoulders to become heavy, cross your arms, and look down at your feet. As a bonus, bite your lip lightly while shuffling your feet.

How do you feel in this position? What happens to your self-confidence now? Go back and forth between these two poses and pay attention to the words you're using to yourself and how you feel differently as you move from one pose to another.

Now, imagine yourself walking into a social setting and seeing a stranger standing tall, smiling warmly, and making eye contact with you. What kind of assumptions will you make about that person solely based on how they are presenting themselves with their body? Will you see them as confident, friendly, and approachable?

Next, imagine shifting your eyes and seeing someone else sitting by herself on a bench with her head held down and her arms folded firmly across her chest. What assumptions will you make of her? Does she appear confident, friendly, or approachable?

Now, think about the people whom you thought were so lucky because they seemed confident, easygoing, and well-liked. How do they look? How do they hold their body?

To appear more confident and easygoing, all you have to do is use the Inner Superpower of Your Body. Your body affects not only how you feel about yourself but also how others see you and the impression they make of you.

You have the power to take control and run your positive and successful body's program whenever you want to. It's as simple as the exercise you just went through. When you take on a powerful pose when you're anxious, it confuses your mind because this is not your body's program for anxiety.

REMEMBER: When your mind and body are not running the same program, your mind gets confused. When your mind gets confused, it lets go of that current emotion. You are then free to choose a new emotion that better suits your needs at that moment.

The net result is that you get to break the cycle of feeling like a victim to your emotions and instead reclaim your true power at the moment.

The next time you go into a situation that causes you fear or self-doubt, use the Inner Superpower of Your Body. Instead of slouching in your chair, looking down at the table, and wringing your hands as you're sitting in class, anxiously waiting for your turn to give your presentation, sit up straight.

Use the Inner Superpower of Your Body to relax your shoulders and allow them to drop comfortably. Uncross your legs, turn your knees outward, and plant your feet firmly on the ground. Look directly ahead of you or at the line where the wall and ceiling meet.

The simple act of focusing your energy and attention on keeping your body open and strong will break your negative emotional state and help you to look and feel a sense of confidence instantly. You can then choose the Word Filters you want to create the experience you're looking for.

Self-Reflection

Spend a few minutes answering these questions and coming up with examples for the following:

1. When you are nervous, scared, or tense, how does your body naturally react?

_____

_____

_____

_____

_____

_____

_____

_____

2. When you feel good about something you've just done, or about yourself, how does your body naturally react?

_____

_____

_____

_____

_____

_____

_____

3. Share two specific examples where your body closed up and caused you to feel even worse about your situation.

_____

_____

_____

_____

_____

_____

_____

_____

_____

_____

4. Share two specific examples where your body opened up and caused you to feel good about your situation.

_____

_____

_____

_____

_____

_____

_____

_____

_____

_____

_____

5. Think about the people you admire. How do they hold their body in stressful situations? What could you learn from them?

_____

_____

_____

_____

_____

_____

_____

_____

_____

_____

6. Think about the people you admire. How do they look that tells you they are comfortable with themselves? What could you learn from them?

_____

_____

_____

_____

_____

_____

_____

_____

_____

_____

_____

_____

CHAPTER 4

The Power of Imagination

For a moment, think about an early childhood memory when you spent numerous hours playing with your imaginary best friend, having fun in your imaginary land, and doing exactly what you wanted to do.

If you didn't have an imaginary friend, think of a time when you were reading a great book and got completely lost in a make-believe land or immersed in the adventures you were reading about. Or maybe think of a time when you were sick in bed and instead of being bored, you used your imagination and turned your bedroom into a jungle gym or a space station ready to blast into outer space!

Stop reading this book for a few minutes; as vividly as you can, bring back one or more memories of a fun childhood experience. Take your time doing this exercise so you can get the full experience of this next Inner Superpower.

Check in with yourself. As you imagine these events from your past, how do you feel? How is your body positioned? If you took the time to vividly recall one of those wonderful memories, chances are you're feeling a little light-hearted, the fun memories are bringing a smile to your face, and your body is naturally open.

You might not have known it when you were younger, but in those moments, you were using your Inner Superpower of Imagination to create your own amusement and entertain yourself. You were also using your Inner Superpower of Imagination to recall those wonderful memories just now.

Why Imagination Is A Superpower

Imagination helps you to entertain yourself, but what is imagination exactly, and what else is imagination good for?

Imagination[3] is defined as "the act or power of forming a mental image of something not present to the senses or never before wholly perceived in reality." It is also defined as "the ability to confront and deal with a problem," and "a creation of the mind."

Based on these definitions, you can see why Imagination is an Inner Superpower. With your imagination, you have the ability to create mental images of something that doesn't even exist in reality— something no one may have ever seen or even thought of before!

With your imagination, you can create endless journeys and adventures that entertain you and bring you excitement and happiness. Imagination gives you the ability to look at different angles of problems and come up with alternative solutions that satisfy you.

---

[3] "imagination." Merriam-Webster.com. 2017.
https://www.merriam-webster.com (7 November 2017).

When you tap into your Inner Superpower of Imagination, you have the ability to fill your life with fun activities that bring you joy and creative solutions that fills you with a sense of adventure or accomplishment. You use your imagination all day, but probably thought little about how incredible your imagination is. You might even downplay the powers of your imagination with, "I don't have a good imagination," or "It's only in my imagination."

If you think you don't have a good imagination, you are giving your subconscious mind the command, "Make sure to look for evidence that I'm not imaginative." Being your loyal assistant, your subconscious mind kicks in to give you the experience you just requested.

You were born with this precious gift and you have a great imagination. If you didn't have a good imagination, you wouldn't be able to recall past events. It's with your imagination that you're able to "see" your friend's face or feel their warm embrace long after you have parted ways. It's your imagination that helps you decide how to solve fun things, such as puzzles or games, to more serious things such as how to patch things up after you've hurt someone.

You have been using your imagination and the power of your mind all along. You just didn't know how powerful your imagination is, nor how to use it consistently to create the results you want. But that's about to change.

How to Destroy Fear and Self-Doubt Using the Power of Your Imagination

Did you know that it is entirely possible to destroy your fear and self-doubt by tapping into the Inner Superpower of Imagination? From her studies[4], Dr. Stephanie Carlson, a prominent scientist who specializes in researching how our brains work, determined that with repetition, you can become the person you pretend to be. What this means is that if you want to be confident, you can become confident by pretending to be confident. To pretend, you have to use your Inner Superpower of Imagination.

Remember, one definition of imagination is "forming a mental image of something not present or never before wholly perceived in reality." When you imagine yourself confident, you are just forming a mental image of yourself in a way that you haven't been before (or haven't consistently been before.)

Think of all the amazing things in your life that you enjoy so much, such as your smartphone, a game console, or even your favorite shoes. For those things to come into reality for you to enjoy, someone had to first imagine them. And not only does someone have to imagine them, but they also have to imagine them in a positive way, a way that brings excitement into that project. Without imagination, nothing would ever get created.

---

[4] Carlson, Stephanie M. et al Evidence for a relation between executive function and pretense representation in preschool children. (2014) https://www.ncbi.nlm.nih.gov/pmc/articles/PMC3864685/

It is no different for you. If you want to be a certain way, you can use your imagination to bring that version of yourself to life. You can use the power of your imagination to see yourself as a fully confident version of yourself.

How do you look? What are you saying? Who are you with? What are you doing? You can use your imagination to vividly see yourself going after what you want with confidence and achieving your goals with ease. Notice how good it feels to just imagine that possibility.

Here's another fun detail about your subconscious mind that helps you bring the things you imagine into real life:

Your subconscious mind doesn't know the difference between real or imagined events. To your subconscious mind, your real or imagined events are just programs. As a program, it's either on or off.

If you're thinking it, feeling it, or doing something, your subconscious mind will view it as a current event that is happening at that moment.

When you vividly imagine yourself tackling a problem with confidence repeatedly, your subconscious mind will believe that you have been successful at tackling that problem with confidence many times. If you have been successful in overcoming a problem ten or twenty times, will you still have the fear or self-doubt the next time you face that problem?

Not likely.

However, if there is still some doubt, you can change that by imagining the successful completion of that task easily and with confidence another twenty—or hundred—times.

Here's another fact about your subconscious mind that is important to create your desired outcome. In an earlier chapter, you learned that your subconscious mind is very literal and will obey your command in the easiest, quickest way possible. When you use the power of your imagination, be sure to use present-tense terms.

This looks like: "I am confident in who I am," instead of "Once I'm confident in who I am, I will..."

When you say and imagine, "I am confident in who I am," you bring your goals of being confident into the present moment. Your subconscious mind will hear and obey the command: "I am confident now. Give me the experience of being confident now."

When you say, "Once I'm confident in who I am, I will..." you're telling your subconscious mind, "Give me the experience of being confident... someday. I want to be confident at some point in the future."

You might say, "I'm OK with being confident someday. It doesn't have to be today." While that's fine to feel that way, imagine what it would be like to take control and change now.

Besides, your subconscious mind will need you to give this command consistently to rewrite your old programming. Now is the perfect time to take those first steps in making your permanent change.

Am I a Fraud?

I'm sure you have heard the expression, "Fake it till you make it." There's a lot of truth to that statement according to Dr. Stephanie Carlson's research[5]. However, for many people, the idea of faking something or pretending to be someone they're not, feels dishonest and wrong.

Many times, I've heard clients say, "I don't want to lie to myself. That is just not right." or "I feel silly pretending to be someone I'm not." When you fake it till you make it, you can look at it as "pretending, lying, or deceiving," or you can look at it as "practicing."

When you go to the gym and work out with weights, are you tricking your body into developing muscles? Of course, you're not! You are actively participating in activities that result in your muscles being developed. You are, practicing with weights to strengthen and build your physical muscles.

Imagination is a mental muscle. Instead of thinking of it as tricking yourself or lying to yourself, how about changing those Word Filters to "practicing," "strengthening," or "developing" your mental muscles? Doesn't it feel good to actively engage in developing your physical muscles?

You can look at your mental muscles the same way and allow yourself to feel good each time you practice this new skill. With repetition, your beliefs become

---

[5] Carlson, Stephanie M. et al Evidence for a relation between executive function and pretense representation in preschool children. (2014) https://www.ncbi.nlm.nih.gov/pmc/articles/PMC3864685/

stronger and more developed, and your brain chemistry changes to match.

Your Personal Creation Studio

Here's a fun way to view your imagination. Think of your imagination as your Personal Creation Studio, or "Studio" for short. Your Studio is your private playground, a place that is safe for you to test out and practice anything you want to develop, whether that's a skill or a thing you want to create.

If you want to develop a certain trait or create a new thing, you can go into your Studio and try out different ways of bringing that goal to life. The cool thing about your Studio is that it's your own private place where you are free to try and try again until you're happy with your result.

In your Studio, there is no pressure; there is no judgment. If you get a result you don't like, you can adjust different aspects of it, or you can scrap it altogether. Your Studio is equipped with a "do-over" button that you can use as many times as you want. You have full control of what happens here!

Let's say you have a fear of talking in front of a group of people and you want to change that. You can start by going to your Studio and practicing visualizing yourself walking up to a group of people, smiling, and saying "hi." Imagine the people you've just approached smiling and saying "hi" back. Do that a few times to feel more comfortable.

Next, imagine yourself standing in a group and being fully present. This means you're not in your head, trying to come up with things to say. Rather, you are there, listening to the conversation and enjoying the moment.

Now, imagine yourself adding to the conversation and imagine the people responding back positively. If you imagine these scenarios repeatedly and you feel good when you imagine them, how do you think you'll be different in a real social setting?

Here's a hint that will help you be successful in social situations. When you are actively listening to a conversation, it is much easier to have something to say because you are hearing what is being said and can respond appropriately.

When you're in your head, thinking about what to say, it feels forced and unnatural. By the time you come up with something to say, the conversation has already moved on and what you came up with may no longer be appropriate, making you look or feel awkward.

REMEMBER: *Your subconscious mind doesn't know the difference between real or imagined events.*

If you're in your head, thinking about being laughed at for saying the wrong thing, your subconscious mind will think you just, in fact, had that experience.

Similarly, if you took the time to imagine yourself at ease and having fun in a social situation twenty times, your subconscious mind would believe that you had fun in a social situation twenty times—twenty actual events where you were at ease and confident while hanging out with others.

When you actually interact with a group the first time in real life, your subconscious mind will think this is the twenty-first time that you've interacted in a group. Since the first twenty times were so wonderful, your subconscious mind has no reason to "protect" you with fear or doubt. Thus, you get to relax and enjoy your time.

With each time you imagine yourself successful, you strengthen your mental muscles and build up the skills necessary for you to be comfortable in a social setting. The best part is you did that all in your Studio, where there are no risks, only opportunities to practice!

The problem is that many people don't understand the enormous power of imagination. Rather than using their Studio to empower themselves, they use it to practice being someone they don't want to be and create scenarios that are damaging to their emotional and physical health.

Before they go into a social situation, they would imagine going to a party where everyone knows each other, and they are the only one who doesn't know anyone. Or they might imagine themselves being the only one who is nervous and awkwardly saying the wrong things and being laughed at or ignored.

This, of course, causes negative thinking, which further increases their fear, anxiety, and self-doubt. By the time they get into that social situation, their anxiety level is so high that they do, in fact, look and act awkward. Their body closes in, they shift uncomfortably, and they can't make eye contact with people.

Similarly, some people spend so much time in their Studio reliving past painful events that it causes them to experience physical symptoms of stress. This pattern of negative thinking interferes with their sleep, their ability to focus, and decreases the overall quality of their lives. They created all of this because they didn't understand the power of their imagination. Anytime you catch yourself creating unwelcomed situations in your Studio, know that you have the power to stop that now. You can change your negative thinking into empowering thoughts.

Remember, your subconscious mind is always paying attention to your commands. When you think or feel a certain way (and you do this using your imagination), your subconscious mind will do all it can to give you the experience you're creating in your Studio.

Your imagination has a very important and vital role in helping you solve problems and be happy. When you actively engage your Inner Superpower of Imagination and use your Studio to practice being the person you want to be, you will change how you feel about yourself and how you feel about your world. You will see problems from different angles and come up with new ways to approach and solve those problems.

Here's a key point to remember:

In every situation, you have to focus your energy and attention on something, whether that's a negative, neutral, or positive aspect of that event. Your mind cannot be completely blank. Why not focus your attention on something that will make life easier and more fun for yourself?

Self-Reflection

Spend a few minutes answering these questions and coming up with examples for the following:

1. Think of the last time you actively engaged the power of your imagination, whether by watching a movie, reading a book, or just creating something great in your mind. How did you feel?

_____

_____

_____

_____

_____

_____

_____

2. Think of a time where you allowed the power of your imagination to get the best of you and become fearful or full of self-doubt. What were you imagining? How did you feel?

_____

_____

_____

_____

_____

3. Go into your studio and come up with two different ways you can think about the situation you just mentioned. Remember to engage your Inner Superpowers of word and your body along with your imagination to create new, powerful scenarios. Have fun in your studio. Your new scenarios could involve fairies, werewolves, unicorns, and superheroes if you like. Remember, this is your private playground. Have fun and tap into your imagination. How do you feel now, having imagined the situation in a different and positive light?

_____

_____

_____

_____

_____

_____

_____

_____

_____

_____

_____

_____

_____

_____

_____

_____

_____

CHAPTER 5

The Power of Courage

When you think of the word "courage" and someone who is courageous, what comes to mind? Who comes to mind? Do you envision someone jumping out of an airplane into enemy territories in the middle of the night? Do you imagine someone scaling a towering, icy mountain or scuba diving with sharks hundreds of feet below? Do you think of someone standing up against a group of hostile people, pushing back and fighting for social change or human justice?

For many, this is how they view courage. To be courageous, many think they must accomplish a nearly impossible task filled with risks of personal injury or even death. It's these epic events that get celebrated in the media and talked about non-stop around the dinner table or among a group of friends.

When compared to these courageous heroes, many people feel bad about themselves because they have trouble thinking about getting out of bed and facing the day, let alone taking those types of enormous risks. Too many people get trapped in this way of thinking, which causes self-doubt, fear, and negative self-judgment.

Maybe you are caught in this pattern, too, and you don't know how to stop feeling bad about yourself or your situation. Once you understand true courage and how to tap into your Inner Superpower of Courage, how you view yourself and what you are capable of will dramatically change for the better.

Why Courage is a Superpower

Courage[6] is defined as "the ability to do something that frightens one," and "the mental or moral strength to venture, persevere, and withstand danger, fear, or difficulty."

Simply put, courage is the strength and ability to face something that YOU see as frightening, difficult, or dangerous. To be courageous, you do not need to climb Mount Everest, tame wild beasts, or stand up against a firing squad. To be courageous, you only need to stand up and face the things YOU are afraid of and find difficult.

Based on these definitions, you are courageous. You are much more courageous than you've realized and much more courageous than you've given yourself credit for. In the words of Nobel Peace Prize winner

---

[6] "courage." Merriam-Webster.com. 2017. https://www.merriam-webster.com (7 November 2017).

Nelson Mandela, "I learned that courage was not the absence of fear, but the triumph over it.[7]"

Think about that statement and then think about the countless times you took a step toward something that completely frightened YOU.

How about that time you could finally strike up a conversation with someone you found intimidating? Maybe your heart pounded rapidly, and you stumbled on your words, but you did it. And even if the results may not have been what you wanted; the fact is that you found the courage to face your fear at that moment.

What about the time you stood your ground and said what you wanted to say? Yes, it was scary, and perhaps you might have even second-guessed yourself for speaking your mind, but the fact is you did. You courageously did it! You looked directly at your fear and went for it! This, in and of itself, is an incredible act of courage that went unnoticed by the world around you—and it probably even went unnoticed by you.

You have been courageous so many times in your life, but you just haven't given yourself the proper credit and acknowledgment. You don't have to let these incredibly courageous moments go unnoticed anymore. You can recognize them, celebrate them, and in doing so, increase your connection to your courage and how often you engage this Inner Superpower throughout your day.

Each tiny, seemingly insignificant act of courage you undertake strengthens your self-belief and stretches

---

7

https://www.brainyquote.com/quotes/quotes/n/nelsonmand178789.html

the boundaries of who you are a little more. When you start to notice and celebrate these wins, however small they might be, you feel good about yourself.

Remember, your subconscious mind is always paying attention to your thoughts and feelings to know what type of experiences you are looking for. When you celebrate these wins, your mind takes notice. It will look for more evidence to show you just how courageous and capable you really are.

You feel more self-assured. You begin to see yourself differently. You start to think and act differently. You allow yourself to take more chances and do the things you want to do because you trust yourself more.

The courage and confidence that grow out of these seemingly unimportant events begin to take shape. You become more and more comfortable challenging yourself and pushing yourself to achieve even greater goals. The things you once thought were big roadblocks become possible and your goals for even greater success are now within reach.

Courage opens up your world; the possibilities are endless. True courage is acting when you feel fear and it is also listening to and following your heart. Courage is accepting yourself exactly as you are. Courage allows you to push through when life gets tough. Courage allows you to connect to others in a deep and meaningful way.

It takes courage—lots of it—to allow others to see your vulnerabilities, your scars, and your quirks. It takes courage to dream big and pursue that dream until it becomes a reality. It takes courage to move on from

uations or people that are toxic and unhealthy for
)u.

When you tap into your Inner Superpower of
)urage and face your fear, you become unstoppable.

Iow to Destroy Fear and Self-Doubt Using the Power of Courage

any people have so much fear and self-doubt that
ey can't relax and be themselves. They work hard to
oid the people and situations they are frightened of.
iey are always on high alert, watching their
vironment, looking for danger. They continuously try
be the person they think others want them to be. This
instant need to be vigilant about their situation and
e self-imposed need to figure out who they need to be
each moment amplifies their fear and self-doubt.

Imagine having to guess what each person expects
)m you and then trying to act in such a way to meet
eir expectations with every interaction you have.
)w exhausting would that be?

With each person you try to impress, you pretend to
: the person you think they want you to be, and you
se a little more of yourself. Soon, you lose connection
who you really are and the beauty and uniqueness
at is you fade away. This leaves you even more
infused about who you are. How can you be confident
d courageous when you don't even know who you
e and what you stand for?

The same goes for always being on guard for
itential situations that could bring you pain or

disappointment. Imagine not being able to relax in any situation because you are continually looking for your escape route. Instead of being present and enjoying each moment, you stay trapped inside your head, thinking of all the things that could go wrong so you could "prepare" yourself. The harder you try to control your environment and those around you, the less you feel comfortable in your own skin and the more fear and self-doubt you'll create.

When you practice acts of courage, you can eliminate the need to control your environment and the need to change yourself to please others. Courage will allow you to be yourself and to be genuinely comfortable in your own skin.

Here's a little fact you may not know about that will instantly help you live more courageously:

Fear exists only in your imagination.
Fear is created by recalling events from
the past or imagining events in the
future. Fear does not exist in the present
moment.

Therefore, if you turn all of your attention on being in the present moment, you instantly eliminate your fear.

"Wait!" you say. "I'm always afraid. Fear is with me every moment, even in the present moment!"

Let's look at those statements a bit to see if they are really true. First, think of the last time you were fearful. What thoughts were running through your mind? Let's

etend that you had a class presentation, and you were
raid. You probably had some, if not all, of these
oughts:

1. I will be so nervous.
2. I will forget what I need to say.
3. I will make a fool of myself.
4. People will laugh at me.
5. I will get a bad grade.
6. I'm terrible at public speaking.
7. I've made a fool of myself in the past.
8. I'm just too scared.

Let's look at the first five statements. These
itements are based in the future. These are things you
e afraid of and you're hoping to avoid them in your
ture.

Statements six and seven are based on your past
periences. You believe you are a terrible public
eaker because of how you presented in the past and
u view that event as you are making a fool of
urself.

You might say that statement eight is based on the
esent moment and you are somewhat correct. "I AM"
a present-tense statement; however, when you go
eper and ask, "why are you scared?" the answer will
her be based on a future event ("I'm scared because I
ight fail.") or based on your past experiences ("I'm
ared because I've done poorly in the past.").

Instead of letting your past experiences and fear of
e future control your reactions, what if you tapped
to your Inner Superpower of Courage to stay in the
esent? It takes courage to let go of old familiar
tterns and start down a new, unknown path.

As you're sitting in your chair, waiting for your turn to present, instead of entertaining those old fearful thoughts, what if you just focused on the moment? Maybe your classmate, Amie, is giving her presentation and you focus all of your attention on what she's saying. Maybe Amie is wearing a shirt with a cool pattern, and you spend your time mentally tracing the outline of that pattern.

Maybe you can spend your time taking slow, deliberate breaths and focusing on your Inner Superpower of Words to boost yourself up or opening up your body to stay calm and confident. Maybe you use your Inner Superpower of Imagination and mentally practice delivering your presentation with confidence. When you courageously stop the old chatter in your mind and do something positive for yourself, you'll improve your outcome drastically.

Remember, having courage does not mean that you have no fear. Rather, it means looking at your fears and taking actions to overcome them. The best way to strengthen your Inner Superpower of Courage is by doing something courageous.

It might seem very counter-intuitive to say, "I don't have the courage to do the things I want to do, but I will do it anyway because I want to be courageous."

You might think, "That's easy for you to say because you don't have my problem. You don't know what it's like to be me and live with my fear. You don't know how much I've already suffered."

While it is completely true that I do not know your unique circumstances, I do know that we all struggle with our own challenges, fear, and self-doubt. I also

ow that courage is a skill that you can learn to master
th patience and practice. I'm not suggesting that you
ke your biggest fear and tackle it head-on. That
ethod might backfire and reinforce your belief that
ur fear is justified and impossible to overcome.

Courage is another mental muscle. It gets better with
nstant use. To exercise your muscles for courage,
art small and build your courage muscles up along the
ay. Find little ways to push yourself or expose
urself to new things every day. It might feel
kward at first to do something outside of your
mfort zone. The more you continue to push past your
mfort zone, the more your comfort zone will expand.

Let's say that singing is a passion of yours and
mething that you're really good at. You may want to
rsue this as a career, but the idea of performing in
nt of others terrifies you. What small steps could
u take to overcome your fear?

Perhaps the first step is singing a few songs to your
mily. Perhaps it's singing to a group of your close
ends. For some, it's easier to do the thing they are
raid of with people they don't know. If this is you,
aybe you can look for opportunities to sing to a small
oup of strangers? Could you look for opportunities to
ng at a daycare or a nursing home? Gradually
crease the size of the group and the duration of your
rformance until you feel at ease performing for an
dience.

*REMEMBER: You can practice and
perfect all of your courageous acts
within the safety of your Studio before
doing it in real life.*

With continued practice, courageous acts will become second nature to you and your confidence will become more and more obvious in the way you live.

Self-Reflection

)end a few minutes answering these questions and
ming up with examples for the following:

Think of three different times where you were acting
urageous but did not give yourself the proper credit.
rite down all the relevant details.

_____

_____

_____

_____

_____

_____

_____

_____

_____

As you consider the events you wrote about in
estion one through the lens of courage, how did it
ake you feel differently?

_____

_____

_____

_____

3. Think about each event again individually. For each event, is there something you wished you would have done or said differently? Write those things down.

_____

_____

_____

_____

_____

_____

_____

_____

_____

_____

_____

_____

_____

_____

_____

_____

_____

_____

4. Next, pick one of those events to practice with. Imagine going into your Studio and reacting the way you wish you had. Practice this way of being repeatedly until it feels comfortable to you. This exercise will help you to react in this way in your future. Feel free to practice reacting the way you want with the other events, too.

CHAPTER 6

The Power of Forgiveness

How often do think about the times you were hurt, mistreated, or rejected by others? When you replayed those events in your mind, how d it make you feel? What emotions came up for you?

Chances are when you thought of these events, you lt several strong emotions such as sadness, fear, hurt, sappointment, betrayal, inferiority, anger, werlessness, loneliness, shame, or other equally gative feelings. Has it ever helped you to feel this ıy? For most people, the answer is "no."

In fact, you've probably experienced having your itire day ruined, not because of what happened that y, but because you spent so much time and energy eling sorry for yourself or beating yourself up for ıat you should have or could have done differently. ɔu wish you could let things go easily like others ound you, but you can't seem to stop thinking about ıat happened and how people have hurt you. How can you forgive and move on when you can't stop reliving the pain in your head?

You are not alone in this pattern. As humans, it's easy for us to focus on and replay negative events. In fact, we are wired that way. Our life experiences have taught us to pay extra attention to negativities and hang on to the pain associated with them.

Ever since you were a little child, you have watched the people around you giving more attention to negative events and giving you the impression that negative events are worth paying special attention to.

Think about it for a moment.

There were countless times where you were happy playing by yourself, and no one took notice. But the moment you hurt yourself, hurt someone else, or did something "bad" like throwing a tantrum, everyone around you rushed in to give you extra attention. Yes, some of that attention was negative, but it's still attention all the same.

Further, when something terrible happens, people talk about it more. If it's newsworthy, every channel on TV will broadcast the story repeatedly. You can't seem to get away from the story no matter how many times you've changed the channel.

Whether or not you know it, events like these cause your subconscious mind to develop beliefs such as, "When I get hurt or do something bad, I get extra attention," or "Pain, trauma, and other unfortunate events are important. Pay attention to them." So, when something goes wrong or when someone hurts you, you hang onto those memories and replay them often.

Think of a time when you had a horrible experience a restaurant. How many people did you share that perience with? What about a time when your staurant experience was just so-so? How many ople did you share that experience with? More likely, u told at least twice as many people about the gative experience as compared to the OK experience.

When you think about those two restaurant amples, how many details can you recall about each cidence? You are likely to recall many details from e terrible experience and not so many things about e so-so experience. This is because your mind is red to pay attention to and remember negative ents.

Remember your friend and assistant, the bconscious mind? It has a vital role in keeping inful memories fresh in your mind. Since its job is to ep you safe from danger (real or imagined), your bconscious mind will not only remember all of your inful experiences, but it will also continuously scan ur surroundings for evidence of similar wrong doings prompt you to avoid certain people and situations.

Sadly, this causes you to be hypersensitive to each stance where you perceive that people might mistreat u, or when you think you are doing something vrong." This often leads you to misread situations and eates unnecessary pain for you.

Why Forgiveness is a Superpower

Stress is the number one cause of so many health problems, such as high blood pressure, stomach problems, headaches, and depression. When you carry so much fear, doubt, or anger, whether at yourself or others, your stress level increases, and it affects your overall health.

> *Forgiveness is a key to lowering your stress and improving your quality of life.*

Forgiveness liberates you from all that heavy burden (and subsequent stress) while providing you with a clean slate to move forward.

Imagine this scenario for a moment. You just got into a terrible argument with a good friend, and you feel like she was mean and hurtful to you. You tried to explain to her why you're feeling hurt and upset, but she just doesn't seem to get it. You become angrier as you withdraw inside yourself. Your friend is trying to make light of the situation and says, "Stop being so sensitive. Come to my party tonight. We'll have so much fun."

If you're hanging on to the hurt, chances are you would choose to stay home and not attend her party. You might even think, "I'm going to send her a clear message about how angry I am by not showing up to her stupid party."

So, instead of going to the party and having fun like you really wanted to, you stayed home and stewed in your anger and misery. Your friend, on the other hand, proceeded to have a great time at her party. She might think about you briefly and she might even feel sad for a moment that you're not there, but she most likely will be focused on the friends who are there and enjoying her time with them.

You wanted to make her pay, but in the end, who really suffered? You were so wrapped up in your pain and thoughts of making her pay that you couldn't enjoy yourself. You replayed the fight over and over, which caused you to be even more upset with your friend. You might even become so irritable that you yelled at your little brother when he asked you to play with him. You are now the one dishing out the pain and you didn't even realize it. How damaging is that?

Let's imagine that you decided to forgive your friend instead. It might feel a little awkward at first because you're not used to letting things go easily. However, because you have learned how to unleash some of your Inner Superpowers, you went into your Personal Creation Studio and practice these new skills.

For thirty minutes straight, you practiced hanging out with your friend at her party, being fully present, and having fun. You practiced seeing yourself completely at ease, laughing with and connecting deeply with this friend and other friends at her party. As you practiced these new skills in your Studio, you also practiced a new ISP Command: "It's easy for me to forgive."

With these practices, you began to feel better about the situation and decided to attend her party. At the party, you noticed how much easier it was for you to have fun. Your friend was thrilled that you attended the party. She gave you a big hug and thanked you for being there.

You leave the party feeling good about yourself and your friendship, and you bring that wonderful energy home with you. When your little brother asks you to play with him, you do so happily, and you two share a precious bonding moment.

Inspirational author Katherine Ponder[8] said something that I very much agree with, "When you hold resentment toward another, you are bound to that person or condition by an emotional link that is stronger than steel. Forgiveness is the only way to dissolve that link and get free."

When you choose to forgive, you stop wasting your time and energy rehashing the same old story and feeling sorry for yourself. That's the power of forgiveness.

REMEMBER: *When you forgive, you set yourself free to enjoy the things that matter most to you.*

You might think, "OK, that makes sense, but what if I forgive someone and they don't change because they think I'm OK with what they did? Or worse yet, what if

---

[8] http://www.azquotes.com/author/20507-Catherine_Ponder

forgive them and they think I'm weak and they take vantage of me even more? I don't want to be friends ith someone like that."

While it's understandable that you might have these ncerns, would you agree that these concerns are fear-sed? If you want to destroy your fear and self-doubt, u can choose to shift your energy away from the miliar fear-based thoughts and focus on your Inner perpowers instead.

When you forgive, it doesn't mean that you have reed with what happened, nor does it mean that u've excused their actions. All it means is that u've accepted that the situation occurred and there's thing you can do to change the past, so you're oosing to focus on the present moment and the ture.

Maybe it's a simple misunderstanding and you can ickly clear things up by having a meaningful nversation that deepens your relationship. Maybe ere's a great lesson or two that you can learn from to lp you grow as a person. When you forgive, the act forgiveness is really for you and not so much for the her person.

Yes, it would be nice if they can understand what ey did and change their future behavior because of it. owever, the decision to change is entirely up to them. ou have no control over that, regardless of how much ne, energy, and effort you spend trying to make it ppen. The more you try to control or manipulate the uation, the longer you stay trapped and bound to this rson. It's almost as if you gave them the power to ntrol how you feel.

Instead, you can forgive that person and move forward. In doing so, you reclaim your power. It's like you're declaring, "Enough! You can't control me anymore. I'm in charge of how I feel and how I spend my time."

Forgiveness also doesn't mean that you have to be friends with that person. Just as the other person has the choice whether to change, you have a choice in whether you want to maintain that relationship. Forgiveness just means letting go of the negativity so you can move forward, with or without that person in your life.

So far, we've been talking about forgiving others and how that frees you. Let's talk about another side of forgiveness that is equally important, but often overlooked, and that's self-forgiveness.

For a moment, think of something you did that you still feel regret, guilt, or shame about. Or maybe think of a time when you let yourself or someone else down, or somehow disappointed yourself. How do these events and the feelings attached to them hold you back? Does it feel heavy and burdensome to carry all of those self-judgments around with you? Wouldn't it be nice to start fresh and move forward without that burden?

If you want a fresh start, you can begin by forgiving yourself. Just like forgiving others, forgiving yourself does not mean that you are OK with what you did. Self-forgiveness means you've recognized that what you did was not desirable and you're willing to let it go so you can spend your energy on discovering ways to improve that situation or make up with someone that you may have hurt.

How to Destroy Fear and Self-Doubt Using the Power of Forgiveness

How does forgiveness help you destroy your fear and self-doubt? Holding onto feelings of hurt, anger, or resentment only makes you feel worse about yourself and your situation and ultimately causes you to second-guess and doubt yourself. You might feel like a victim. You might feel all alone in this world. It's no wonder that you would want to protect yourself from future pain.

But what happens when you try to defend yourself? Usually, self-protection means thinking about and remembering the act that caused you pain, hoping to avoid a repeat event. It also means having to close yourself up to some degree.

Maybe you've been rejected or betrayed by a friend, and now, you're afraid to open up and let people get to know the real you. Perhaps you've been teased by others for expressing yourself, so now, you hold back from saying what you want to say. Perhaps you've failed at something important to you and now, you no longer attempt to take on meaningful challenges out of fear of repeating the failure.

Let's say you've been picked on by a classmate and now, you're afraid to be around that person. What thoughts do you have when that person is near you? Do you show up as a happy, confident, and carefree person? Or do you show up as angry, timid, and awkward? Are you showing up in a way that makes it difficult for someone to tease you, or are you showing up as an "easy target?"

I'm not suggesting that it's your fault that they teased you. You are definitely NOT at fault. Bullies will be bullies, and you cannot control that. What you do have control over is how you feel and how you present yourself to others.

Remember, your subconscious mind is always working to give you more of your current experience. When you focus on how this person has teased you and caused you pain, your subconscious mind will look for evidence of the same. This causes you to be on high alert and fearful.

Remember the chapter about the Inner Superpower of Your Body? In that chapter, you learned that when your mind is running a "weak mind program" such as fear, your body will naturally close up, making you look small and not very confident. These factors work together against you, making it easier for bullies to continue to pick on you. The good news is that you can change this pattern.

Imagine you've forgiven the person who picked on you and let go of the negativities. Rather than taking what they said or did personally, you recognize that this person is dealing with their own stuff and was just taking it out on you. That doesn't make the situation right, but it puts the situation in a different perspective for you, doesn't it? How would you show up differently now? What thoughts would you have?

The next time you see that person, rather than feeling fearful, you might feel neutral or better yet, even compassionate toward them. Because you are no

nger focusing on fear, your mind and your body will
spond appropriately, and you will appear completely
fferent to others.

When you focus your energy on protecting yourself,
u limit your positive energy and limit your ability to
in the present moment.

> **REMEMBER:** *Fear exists only in your*
> *imagination. You create fear by recalling*
> *events from your past or imagining*
> *events in your future. Fear does not exist*
> *in the present moment.*

When you get out of your head and focus on what is
front of you, you eliminate your fear and self-doubt.
hen you don't have to worry so much about how to
t, what to say, or how to protect yourself, you will
el better and stronger overall. Your self-esteem and
nfidence automatically increase. You can relax, be
urself, and enjoy the people around you and the
vironment that you're in.

In addition, forgiveness can help you develop and
engthen your other Inner Superpowers and restore
ur peace of mind. How powerful is that?

NOTE:

Forgiveness work can be challenging for many. While the following exercises are helpful in releasing unwanted emotions, they do not replace professional help. If your situation is difficult to handle, or you don't know how to proceed on your own, please talk to your parents or a trusted adult and ask for help.

You can also do an internet search for "teen crisis" with your city and state for local resources. For example, "teen crisis Asheville, North Carolina."

Self-Reflection

)end a few minutes answering these questions and
ming up with examples for the following:

)rgiving Others

Think of a person or situation that you still hold
ger or resentment for. Write down key relevant
formation. (**NOTE:** Since you will be addressing
ry personal issues with the exercises in this chapter,
)u might want to write your answers in a separate
)tebook or journal.)

_____

_____

_____

_____

_____

_____

_____

_____

_____

_____

_____

_____

_____

2. How has holding on to the negativity and pain from this event holding you back? What has it prevented you from doing? What might it have caused you to do that you otherwise wouldn't have?

_____

_____

_____

_____

_____

_____

3. Are you afraid that something bad would happen if you were to forgive this person or situation? Go ahead and express any fear you might have.

_____

_____

_____

_____

_____

_____

4. How can forgiving this person or situation improve your life? What are you now free to do, think, or feel without the weight of this issue?

_____

_____

_____

_____

_____

_____

Take a moment to notice how liberating it feels to let
of the weight of this problem. With your
rgiveness, you have the power to give yourself this
agnificent gift of freedom to move forward.

rgiving Yourself

Think of something that you've done that you feel
gret, guilt, or shame about. Write down all the
levant details.

_____

_____

_____

_____

_____

_____

_____

_____

_____

_____

_____

_____

_____

_____

_____

_____

_____

_____

_____

_____

_____

_____

_____

2. As you were thinking about and writing down details of that event, how did it make you feel? What thoughts did you have?

_____

_____

_____

_____

_____

_____

_____

3. Why haven't you forgiven yourself?

_____

_____

_____

_____

_____

_____

_____

4. What are you afraid would happen if you forgave yourself?

_____

_____

_____

_____

_____

_____

_____

_____

What can you learn from this event?

_____

_____

_____

_____

_____

_____

_____

_____

_____

How can you use what you've learned to help yourself be a better person?

_____

_____

_____

_____

_____

_____

_____

_____

_____

_____

_____

Spend a few minutes envisioning this improved version of yourself, having learned a powerful lesson. Give yourself permission to embrace this lesson and move forward now.

CHAPTER 7

The Power of Love

L ove is a primary and essential human need.
There are thousands of songs about love. There
are thousands of movies about love. Human
es are conceived as a result of love. Love conquers
. Love makes the world go 'round.

There is no shortage of inspiration for words to
scribe love and the effects of love. Without love and
irturing, we can't thrive. We crave the feeling of
ing loved and we enjoy showing love to those we
re about. Love fills us with a sense of comfort,
longing, and safety. When we have love, life is easier
d more meaningful. When we lack love, life seems
nely and cold.

Let's do a quick check-in on the love you have in
ur life. Stop reading this book and for the next five
inutes, grab a piece of paper and make a list of all the
ople you love. Take the time to create this list before
ntinuing with the rest of this chapter. This is an
iportant step to assessing your Power of Love. Go
ead; grab a piece of paper and a pen or pencil. Set

your timer for five minutes and go! Just create your list freely and write down whoever comes to mind.

Take a look at your list. At what point did you mention yourself? Are you toward the top of your list, somewhere in the middle, or at the very bottom? Did you even make it on your own list?

It is common for people to forget to include themselves on their "People I love" list because they focus their love outwardly. When they think of giving and receiving love, they think it's an act coming from themselves to someone else or from someone else to them.

Others feel uncomfortable with the idea of self-love, fearing they might appear arrogant or self-centered. Still, others feel unlovable or see themselves as being undeserving of self-love.

Where are you on this spectrum? Do you show yourself the same level of kindness, love, and respect that you show others, or do you treat yourself poorly in these areas? Do you make time for yourself as you do for others?

While it's a wonderful trait to love others and to treat others with love, it is equally, if not more important to love yourself.

To fully experience the Power of Love, you need to start from within and develop a strong feeling of love for yourself. In this chapter, when we talk about love, we're talking about self-love. When you love yourself deeply, giving love to and receiving love from others will be a breeze.

Why Love is a Superpower

hen you think of self-love, what is the first thing that
mes to mind? Do you get excited at the thought of
ing able to show yourself how important and
serving you are? Or does the idea of taking the time
care for yourself and your needs feel foreign and
comfortable for you?

If it puts a smile on your face when you think about
owing yourself love, then you're ahead of the curve.
ahead and continue to show yourself just how
agnificent you are!

If it makes you uncomfortable to think of self-love,
t's work together to change that. You deserve to love
urself and treat yourself with respect, kindness, and
mpassion.

Why would something as simple and beneficial as
acticing self-love be so uncommon and difficult for
any? Part of that answer may lie within our culture's
finition of self-love[9]: "1. Conceit 2. Regard for one's
vn happiness or advantage."

Given that part of the definition of self-love is
onceit" and "regard for one's own advantage," it's no
onder so many people are uncomfortable with the
ncept of loving themselves. After all, who wants to
seen as a conceited person or one who only regards
ings for their advantage? Consequently, instead of
owing ourselves love and creating our own

---

[9] "self-love." Merriam-Webster.com. 2017.
ps://www.merriam-webster.com (7 November 2017).

happiness, we give love to others, and we depend on others to give us love and to make us happy.

What if, instead of focusing on those aspects of the definition of self-love, we accepted that self-love is "regard for one's own happiness?"

For the next few minutes, imagine that you have the total freedom to focus on creating your personal happiness. To be clear, when I say, "freedom to focus on creating your personal happiness," I mean freedom to do what you want for yourself, as long as you're not purposefully breaking the law or hurting someone else.

What would that look like for you? How would you think, act, or feel differently when your decisions are based solely on your happiness and not pleasing someone else—nor being concerned about what others may think of how you spend your time? How liberating does it feel to leave behind the fear, self-doubt, negative judgment, regret, shame, and guilt?

That's exactly what self-love can do for you. It can fill you with wonderful feelings that motivate you to live your life to the fullest. At a deep level, we all want to feel loved and to know that we are deserving of love. We all want to be able to show ourselves love; so why is it hard for most people to show self-love?

The following three misguided beliefs are often cited as the reasons why many people are uncomfortable making self-love a priority.

Misguided Beliefs

s Selfish to Focus on Your Needs

Chances are, early in your life, the act of self-love
d doing what makes you happy was very natural to
u. Imagine these scenarios.

You were blissfully minding your own business and
ing what feels good to you, instead of allowing your
ling to pressure you to do what you don't want to
. Your sibling got mad at you and angrily accused
u of being thoughtless, inconsiderate, or selfish.

Maybe another time you were scolded because you
ld your parents you wanted to go to your friend's
use as planned, instead of staying home to babysit
ur siblings. Perhaps your parents yelled at you and
ld you how disappointed they were with you. They
id that a good person would think about others'
elings and would sacrifice their needs to make them
ppy.

Maybe you were told that you should be ashamed of
ways wanting things your way. Guilt, shame, and a
ad of other heavy burdens were placed upon you, and
u learned just how much that hurts.

Your subconscious mind was paying close attention,
it always does. It recorded this whole painful
change, and it will use it to help protect you from
nilar painful experiences in the future. The next time
u think about doing what makes you happy, your
bconscious mind kicks in to protect you and replays
is and other similar movies.

You'll start feeling uneasy as you second-guess yourself with questions such as, "Is what I want really all that important? Am I being thoughtless, inconsiderate, or selfish?"

And as you think about those thoughts and feel the anxiety around them, you decide to do what the other person wanted. And for that, you get rewarded. Your parents told you how proud they are that you're thinking about other people's feelings. They tell you that you're such a good person and rewarded you with extra attention, love, or other tokens of appreciation.

After a few of these incidences, you grew up believing:

- Doing what I want is thoughtless, inconsiderate, and selfish.
- It's more important to make other people happy than to make myself happy.
- When I sacrifice my needs, I am appreciated by others.

You're Not Worthy of Good Things in Life

These beliefs were intensified by other experiences in your life that caused you to feel as though you weren't deserving of good things. Perhaps in the heat of anger, your parents yelled at you to stop wasting time on "useless" things (things that you loved doing) because you should focus on bringing your grades up and helping with chores around the house.

Or maybe you've heard your parents talk about all the sacrifices they have made to provide for you and your siblings, and that made you feel guilty. Maybe a

end or two ended their friendships with you because
ou didn't do what they wanted to do.

Then there were all the times you beat yourself up
r messing up or letting yourself or others down.
xperiences like these reinforced your belief that your
sires and needs are not that important and that you
e not worthy of them. To conform to what others
pect of you and earn the title of being "worthy," you
cus your attention on meeting others' needs while
glecting your own.

When you continue to ignore your own needs, you
se connection to who you are and to what makes you
el good. This causes your self-esteem to plummet and
ur dissatisfaction with yourself (and your life) to
orsen.

ou Are Unlovable Because You Are Flawed

Even when you have the time to focus on your
eds, you may have a hard time showing yourself love
cause you can't stop focusing on your perceived
ws. This causes you to feel unworthy and
deserving of love and happiness.

Here's a common scenario among teens. See if you
n relate to this or a similar situation. There is a
ecial occasion coming up; maybe a school dance or a
end's party, and you're so excited to attend. You
und the perfect outfit and your hair looks great. But
is morning you woke up with a large pimple on your
ce.

Instead of admiring yourself for how great you look
d focusing on the fun event, you focus all of your
ention on the pimple. Instead of being present and

enjoying yourself, you're stuck in your head, thinking about your pimple, which causes you to feel insecure about how you look. At the gathering, you find it hard to enjoy yourself because you're certain that everyone is staring at your pimple and judging you.

If you often feel this way, I have some news for you. You're a human being. As long as you're a human being, you'll have perceived flaws. There's just no way around it. If you wait until you think you are perfect before loving yourself, you'll lose out on an incredible opportunity for happiness and fulfillment right now.

Loving yourself does not mean that you believe you are perfect or that you always do things perfectly. Loving yourself means that you choose to accept yourself exactly as you are, flaws, and all.

REMEMBER: Showing yourself love and being kind to yourself are two of the best things you can do to build your self-confidence and self-esteem and change your life for the better.

When you love yourself, you release the constant pressure of having to make others happy and the heavy burden of living with endless self-doubt and self-judgments.

Without the pressure, doubts, and judgment, you'll have the freedom and peace of mind to explore things you enjoy, which helps you to grow as a person. When you know who you are and you feel good about

urself, it is much easier to make positive decisions
r yourself.

Self-love acts as a natural anti-depressant and a
tural anti-anxiety. The more you love yourself and
at yourself with kindness, the easier it will be to tap
to your strength and stay calm and clear-minded
ring difficult situations.

Self-love also makes bouncing back from these
pes of events easier. When you practice self-love
nsistently, you'll become a happier, healthier person
ith a strong sense of self-worth. Your ability to give
d receive love deepens because you now see yourself
a good person who is deserving of love.

How to Destroy Fear and Self-Doubt Using The Power of Love

r a moment, think about how you've been treating
urself when your fear and self-doubt are high. Have
u been showing yourself love, or have you been
owing disrespect or disregard for yourself? In those
oments, are the words you're using to yourself
pportive and kind, or do you make the situation
orse by calling yourself names and berating yourself
r your perceived flaws?

Think about the words you say to yourself in these
uations. Would you ever say these same words to a
end, a family member, or even a stranger when they
e already down on themselves? Would it be OK to
lk to others this way?

Chances are, if you're honest with yourself, the answer is an easy NO! It is not OK to speak to others the way you speak to yourself when you're upset. If you talk to others the way you talk to yourself, you wouldn't have too many friends. People would think you're mean, abusive, or a bully.

And yet, somehow, you feel it's okay to talk to yourself in this manner. These kinds of self-talk show a big disregard for yourself and reinforce your belief that you are unworthy or undeserving of love. This is not exactly a great foundation for showing yourself love.

Instead of beating yourself up the next time you feel fear or self-doubt, what if you tapped into your Inner Superpower of Words to give yourself love and support? One way you can show yourself love is to challenge yourself to treat yourself with the same level of thoughtfulness, kindness, and respect that you show the person you love most.

If you can't imagine saying any words to this person, avoid saying them to yourself. If it makes you feel good to use these words with that person, start using those words to yourself. You can choose positive Word Filters such as:

- "Slow down. Breathe. You've got it."
- "I believe in you."
- "Everything will be OK."
- "Let's figure out how to solve this problem."
- "You can do it!"

You can also go into your Personal Creation Studio and practice solving whatever problem you're facing with courage, confidence, and self-belief. Use your

ɪagination to vividly see yourself conquering your
oblems in several creative ways.

When you practice trusting yourself and your
ɪlities, your confidence skyrockets. You'll find it
sier to face your problems and follow your dreams
ɪth courage. How you feel about yourself and the
ords you use when you talk to yourself become
ghly positive.

With practice, you'll find it easier to prioritize
ourself and your needs. Your subconscious mind will
ɪlp you achieve your dreams by helping you to focus
ɪ the important aspects of yourself. You can practice
ɪlf-love by forgiving yourself and accepting your
ortcomings while giving yourself permission to see
e best in yourself.

When you show yourself that kind of love, support,
d encouragement, how does it feel? What would you
able to do differently?

Besides showing yourself love in moments of fear
d self-doubt, what if you showed yourself love daily
choosing activities that relax you, inspire you, and
charge you? When you make the conscious decision
nurture your body, heart, and spirit, you leave very
tle room left for fear and self-doubt. If you feel good
out yourself and you see your flaws or failures as
portunities for growth, what is there to be afraid of?

REMEMBER: *When you treat yourself as a person who deserves love, kindness, and respect, you are showing others how to treat you.*

Engaging in self-care activities daily help you to release your stress, gives you more energy, and helps you to look and feel your best so you can be happy with yourself and your life.

Remember to include some self-love activities that might not feel very fun, but that you know are important for your overall health and happiness, such as eating healthy.

Self-Reflection

)end a few minutes answering these questions and
·ming up with examples for the following:

In the beginning of the chapter, you created a list of
ople you love. Did you make it onto your own list?
ɔw did you feel when you discovered that showing
·urself love is just as important as showing love for
·yone else?

_____

_____

_____

Think of a time when you felt upset or disappointed
ith yourself and you used harsh, damaging words as
·u talked to yourself. What words did you use? What
·mes did you call yourself?

_____

_____

_____

How did those words and names make you feel?

_____

_____

_____

_____

4. What was the outcome of that situation? Was it resolved, or does it still linger for you?

_____

_____

_____

_____

_____

_____

5. Now, think about that same situation again; this time, with love and kindness for yourself. Imagine your thoughts and self-talk through these Word Filters. What words did you choose to speak to yourself this time?

_____

_____

_____

_____

_____

6. How do these words make you feel differently?

_____

_____

_____

_____

_____

_____

_____

_____

_____

How do you think the outcome would have been
ıproved if you had spoken to yourself with these
ords when you first encountered this issue?

_____

_____

_____

_____

_____

_____

_____

_____

_____

List two to three things you currently do consistently
show yourself love. They don't need to be grand
stures or even highly time consuming. Using positive
d caring self-talk and allowing yourself to learn
ıen you make mistakes are great examples.

_____

_____

_____

_____

_____

_____

_____

_____

_____

_____

9. Create a list of ten things you could do to show yourself love in the future. Remember, even little things you do that are good for you or allow you the space to feel special are great. Anything counts here, no matter how small or how large, as long as you are showing yourself love in the process.

Example: Eat an apple instead of a bag of chips, take a twenty-minute walk after dinner, listen to music, play with your dog, buy yourself something nice, practice ISP Commands, meditate, etc.

_____

_____

_____

_____

_____

_____

_____

_____

_____

_____

10. Now that you are aware of the Inner Superpower of Love, are you willing to start showing yourself love daily? Make that commitment to yourself now. You can place a sticky note by your phone or nightstand as a daily reminder to engage in this vital self-care activity. You can even wear a special ring or another piece of accessory you like, as a symbol of your commitment to show yourself love each day.

CHAPTER 8

The Power of Perseverance

We all have plans that don't turn out as we intend, dreams that fall apart, and changes that are beyond our control. Setbacks, changes, and obstacles are all a part of life—a part that no one can completely avoid.

How do some people face these tough and ever-changing situations and still come out ahead, while others crumble at the slightest thought of such challenges? What is their secret? How do they keep moving forward when others just want to quit when the pressure becomes higher?

The secret ingredient for the people who keep pushing on when things get tough is perseverance. Some people were born with the ability to persevere, and they can power through even the most challenging situations with seeming ease.

Perseverance is defined as "a steady persistence in a course of action, a purpose, a state, etc., especially in spite of difficulties, obstacles, or discouragement.[10]" How we

---

[10] perseverance." Merriam-Webster.com. 2017.
https www.merriam-webster.com (7 November 2017).

deal with the constant unpredictable events in our lives depends largely on our attitude, our belief systems, and our commitment to ourselves.

Maybe perseverance is not something that comes naturally to you, and the idea of pushing through difficulty sounds downright scary or even impossible to you right now. Luckily for you, perseverance, like all other ISPs, can be learned and strengthened with practice.

Having perseverance can mean the difference between turning your problems into opportunities or allowing your fear and judgments to cause you anxiety and keep you stuck. Given that the average person has challenges and unexpected curveballs thrown at them every day, knowing how to deal with these situations positively will help you move forward rather than becoming held back.

How you view these events will have a significant impact on your quality of life. Instead of seeing your challenges as disasters and wallowing in fear or self-pity, what if you recognized them as opportunities for growth? How would your life be different if you use these challenges as stepping-stones to an even greater success and happiness for yourself?

Why Perseverance Is a Superpower

Did you know that you have persevered through many challenging situations throughout your life? Did you also know that perseverance is actually a very natural part of who you are?

You don't believe me? Let me explain.

When you were an infant, you did not understand how to feed yourself. The first few times you tried to feed your self solid food, you made a complete mess. Chances are you fed your cheeks, chin, nose, and floor more often than you fed your mouth. But you didn't stop, did you? You continued to push forward and look at you! You feed yourself effortlessly, and mostly, you actually put food into your mouth and not on the floor like you once did.

Then, there are those times you tried to learn how to walk. How many times did you work so hard to stand up, only to fall right back down before even taking that first step? You didn't give up then either, did you? You persevered.

There could be several chapters written—or even a whole new book or two—about all the other things that you have pushed through, which allowed you to become a stronger and better person. You do this daily without giving yourself credit or even noticing most of the time.

How would your life look right now if you had decided at eleven months old that walking was too difficult and that you were too scared of falling and getting hurt again? Chances are the freedom of movement that you now enjoy and take for granted as a natural part of your being wouldn't be available to you.

I know this example might seem ridiculous at first, but this situation is not very different from the challenges you may face right now. Think about it. At eleven months old, walking was a very difficult and overwhelming task. Your muscles were not fully developed, nor were they strong enough to support your weight effortlessly. You were just learning how to control your motor skills.

The task of controlling your body that is now so automatic to you required much concentration and effort on your part at eleven months old. It required a tremendous amount of effort to just push yourself up from the floor. In the beginning, each time you got up, you fell right back down.

But you persisted.

And don't forget the countless obstacles—the chairs, the coffee table, the slippery floor—all of which made walking ever so challenging. But each time you fell, you brushed yourself off and tried again. You were determined to figure it out and eventually, you did!

At first, you could only take a wobbly step or two before falling again. But you stayed the course. Soon, your steps became solid, and they rapidly evolved into walking longer distances. Ultimately, you even learned how to run.

You might laugh at this example, but that's the power of your perseverance at work. If you had given up on yourself at eleven months old, your life would have been dramatically different—and in this extreme example, be filled with significant challenges.

Not only does perseverance help you achieve your goals and build your confidence and self-worth, but when you persevere, you become healthier mentally.

Spend a moment thinking about how you were affected by a change, challenge, or setback that you worked hard to avoid. What was that experience like? Did you think about it so much you frequently felt worried, tense, or irritable? When you focused so much of your attention on the thing you wanted to avoid, did you have the mental ability to relax and enjoy yourself? Did you feel so anxious that it was hard for you to focus or to sleep well? How about your relationships? How were they affected when you were filled with stress? How satisfied were you with your life at that moment?

Focusing so much on the problem or what's wrong in your life wreaks havoc on your mental health. When you focus on the present moment and on your strengths, you lessen your stress, and your mental health improves.

I'm not saying that once you've decided to persevere, everything will magically fall into place and become easy. You will still have to put in the work to create the changes you desire and some of the work could be boring or difficult for you.

However, when you face your fear and work toward overcoming your problem, your attitude about it changes. Remember, your subconscious mind is always looking for the next command from you and it will do all it can to give you the experience you ask for.

When you think of a situation as overwhelming or as something scary to run away from, your subconscious mind will scan your environment and focus on all the details that could reinforce your feelings of overwhelm and fear. This will make your situation appear even more intimidating.

What experiences would your subconscious mind help you focus on when you think of the same situation with an attitude of, "I have no idea how to solve this, but I am determined to figure it out!"? In this instance, your subconscious mind would focus your attention on ways to solve your problem. Instead of bringing only challenges or obstacles to your awareness, your subconscious mind starts showing you available options. As you begin to see solutions and possibilities, your stress level drops, and your confidence rises.

Perseverance helps you to focus on the big picture while staying in the present moment. Remember, fear is based on your thoughts of the past or future. Being present helps you to release your fear and self-doubt. You can then relax and focus on your strengths, come up with creative solutions, and be open to and accepting of new opportunities.

Things that used to stress you out and cause problems for you in the past don't have to be problems anymore. They can be a great opportunity for growth if you let them.

REMEMBER: Life will continue to throw you curveballs. How you respond to them will determine your outcome and your satisfaction with life.

How to Destroy Fear and Self-Doubt Using the Power of Perseverance

The good news is that tapping into your Inner Superpower of Perseverance is easier than you think. In fact, if you've read the chapters in this book in order, you already know everything you need to know to persevere.

You can cultivate a strong sense of perseverance just by using the power of words alone. However, when you incorporate all the Inner Superpowers you've learned, this task becomes much easier. All you have to do is practice what you've learned so far and you will succeed.

For the next few minutes, think of an obstacle you're facing that seems difficult to overcome. Pay attention to the thoughts you're having and how they make you feel. Think of all the reasons you've been telling yourself why this obstacle is so difficult to resolve.

Maybe you've attempted to solve it a few times but haven't succeeded. Or perhaps you haven't tried to address this roblem yet because your fear and self-doubt are too high Whatever the reason might be, can you see that may your inability to solve this issue stems from a lack of s f-confidence that prevented you from taking the next step f action and pushing through?

leashing your Inner Superpower of Perseverance start with a powerful mindset of "I believe in myself. I kno I can handle anything that comes my way."

what if you don't believe in yourself and you doubt you bility to handle tough situations? That's OK. Even if you n't fully believe in yourself just yet, know that if you deci d to tap into your Inner Superpowers, you could buil your self-confidence and self-trust.

ce a powerful mindset is the foundation for pers erance and for achieving any goal, you can start out by pping into your Inner Superpower of Words and cho Word Filters that build yourself up. How you think, feel. nd act are direct results of the Word Filters that you cho .

e a step back and look at the whole picture. Examine the ord Filters you have been using when you think about the ituation. How can you change those words to neut lize them and make them non-threatening to you?

attention to how you've been judging yourself and the ople involved. Doesn't it feel heavy and burdensome to c ry those feelings with you? You can release that unn essary weight and give yourself a fresh start by tapp g into your Inner Superpower of Forgiveness.

give yourself for the things you may have done (and the ngs you could have done but didn't do) that you feel cont uted to this situation. Those things are in the past and u can choose a different path moving forward. You can also choose to forgive others and free yourself from that old bond to them that held you back.

Examine the Word Filters you have been using when you think about yourself and your abilities. If you have been using Word Filters that tear you down, you can stop doing that now. Instead, start focusing on your strengths and the things you're good at, even if these things are not related to this particular challenge.

Be kind to yourself by using Word Filters that build up your self-trust, self-confidence, and self-esteem. Tap into your Inner Superpower of Love and do things that relax you, energize you, or motivate you to be your best. Remember to incorporate the Inner Superpower of your Body into your daily life. How you present yourself will strongly influence how you feel about yourself and the situation. Practice holding your body in strong and open positions to increase your confidence.

To persevere, you also need to know your goal. Maybe you don't have the exact outcome in mind and that is fine. You can still take the next step if you know the direction you want to head and have a milestone or two in mind.

Look at the obstacle again. What results do you want to create? Do these results match your values or what's important to you? Do you feel good when you think about achieving these results? Create a plan for overcoming your roadblocks and transforming them into opportunities for growth. Tap into your Inner Superpowers of Courage and Imagination and practice achieving your goal with ease.

Remember, you can practice any of these steps in the safety of your Personal Creation Studio until you feel good about them.

REMEMBER: When you focus on your strengths and take small, consistent steps toward your goals, you'll build up your confidence and your ability to persevere will become stronger every day.

You already know how to persevere. You've been doing this ever since you were an infant. All you have to do is put one foot in front of the other, one baby step at a time, and you will stretch and grow in ways you couldn't have predicted or imagined.

Self-Reflection

Spend a few minutes answering these questions and coming up with examples for the following:

1. Before reading this chapter, did you know that perseverance is a very natural part of who you are and that you have persevered through many challenging situations? How does knowing that make you feel differently about yourself?

_____

_____

_____

_____

_____

2. Think of a time when you faced a challenging or difficult situation, and you gave up. What Word Filters did you use? How did they hold you back?

_____

_____

_____

_____

_____

_____

_____

_____

3. L ok at the Word Filters you wrote for question two. How can you change those words to neutralize them and mak them non-threatening for you?

___ _____

___ _____

___ _____

___ _____

___ _____

___ _____

4. ink about three instances where you persevered desp e challenges. Write the relevant details down.

___ _____

___ _____

___ _____

___ _____

___ _____

___ _____

___ _____

___ _____

___ _____

___ _____

___ _____

___ _____

___ _____

___ _____

___ _____

___ _____

5. Examine the three scenarios you wrote down. What qualities or strength did you embrace that allowed you to keep going? What Word Filters did you use? Write these down. These qualities and strengths will help you persevere in future situations.

_____

_____

_____

_____

_____

_____

_____

_____

_____

_____

_____

_____

_____

_____

_____

_____

_____

_____

_____

_____

_____

_____

B)NUS: *Five Simple Steps to Release Your Unwanted Emotions*

Step)ne: Identify Your Feeling

T take control of your feelings, you must first be able to id itify it. Are you feeling sad, disappointed, irritated, or angi ? Maybe you're feeling insecure, worried, or anxious? Be : specific as you can with your unique feeling and avoi generalizing everything as "mad," "sad," or "bad." Inst(d of saying "mad," get specific. Are you angry, hurt, disa)ointed, or irritated? For this example, let's say you're feel ¿ scared.

Step wo: Rate Your Feeling

C ce you've identified your feeling, rate it on a scale of 0 t(10, with 10 being the strongest it could be. For exar)le: "I feel scared, and it's rated 8 out of 10 (which sho\ you are feeling moderately to severely scared)."

Step hree: Locate Your Feeling

N xt, identify where in your body you physically feel this eling. For example, "I feel scared, and I notice that feel ¿ in my stomach."

Step our: Identify Your Physical Sensation

P / attention to how your body responds and describe the nsation you notice. Maybe you feel some tightness, heav less, or pain. Perhaps it's a dull ache or a burning sens ion. Maybe it feels difficult to breathe, or you feel choked up. For example, "I feel scared. It's rated 8/10, and it feels like a sharp pain in my stomach."

Step Five: Releasing Your Negative Feeling

Your breath is powerful and can help you let go of your negative emotions quickly. Let's use the example of "*I feel scared. It's rated 8/10, and it feels like a sharp pain in my stomach,*" to demonstrate how to release your emotion with your breath.

Start by closing your eyes and for a moment, allow yourself to feel the sharp pain in your stomach. Notice how uncomfortable that sharp pain is. Notice how the sharp pain is holding you back from having a good day.

Then, take a very slow and deliberate deep breath in as you count from one to four. As you're counting slowly, imagine that you are collecting the sharp pain with your breath. Next, hold your breath for a count of four to contain your emotion. Finally, on purpose, choose to release the pain with your exhale. Breathe out fully and loudly, letting that pain go as the air leaves your body.

Take in another slow deep breath in and imagine yourself collecting even more pain. Hold your breath once more for a count of four and again, release the pain by breathing out even more deeply and loudly than before.

After two deep and deliberate breaths, allow your breathing to become easy and natural. With every easy breath you take in, imagine yourself picking up more pain. With every easy breath out, you're choosing to release the pain.

As you continue to breathe easily, collecting and releasing your negative emotion, give yourself these ISP Commands: "I choose to let this pain (insert your negative feeling here) go. It feels good to let this <u>pain</u> (your negative feeling) go. I deserve to let this <u>pain</u> (your negative feeling) go. I deserve to be free (or a different positive emotion of your choice)."

After a minute or so, reevaluate your feelings. How do you feel now? Is that old feeling still there, has it changed into a different feeling, or is it still the same feeling, but much less in intensity? Perhaps it is now a two instead of an eight. You might even find yourself pleasantly surprised to find that old feeling had simply vanished.

If you still have any negative sensations, note its location and rate it again. Then, take another two to three deep breaths just as before, collecting and releasing the negative emotions as you do. Continue this exercise until you no longer feel your negative feeling. Your goal is to be free of the negative feeling and take control of your emotions. In the beginning, it might take you several minutes. However, the more you practice, the faster and easier it will be!

You can use this exercise to release any unwanted emotions, regardless of where they came from, not just when you are practicing your ISP Commands.

About the Author

Dear Reader,

If you are a teenager struggling with high stress, anxiety, self-doubt, low-confidence or depressive symptoms, I want you to know that you are not alone. I know because I have been there myself. My name is Jacqui Letran, and I have over eighteen years of experience helping thousands of teens, and I know I can help you!

I know you're frustrated, scared, and lonely. I was too. I also know confidence, success, and happiness are achievable because I have successfully freed myself from those old emotions and embraced my life with excitement, confidence, and joy. My goal is to help you understand the power of your mind and show you how you can master it to overcome your struggles and step into the magnificence of your own being, just like I did—and just like thousands of others have done using these same techniques.

Who I am and why do I care?

My life was rather easy and carefree until I hit my teenage years. Overnight, it seemed that all my friends transformed from girls into women! They began to wear makeup and dressed in expensive and sexy clothes. They flirted with boys. Some even flaunted the older boys they were dating in front me. I, on the other hand, remained

trap d in my boyish body. And, within the rules of my
supe strict mother, wearing makeup, sexy clothes, or going
on d es were not options for me.

I elt different and isolated—and I quickly lost all my
frier s. I didn't know what to say or how to act around
othe . I felt awkward and left behind. I just didn't fit in
anyr re. I became more and more withdrawn as I
won red what was wrong with me. Why didn't I blossom
into woman like all my friends? Why was life so difficult
and unfair?

- **I blamed my mother for my problems.** "If she weren't so strict, I would be allowed to date and have nice, sexy clothes," I thought. At least then I would fit in, and everything would be perfect!

- **I also felt very angry.** My life had taken a turn for the worst—but no one seemed to care or even notice. I started skipping school, began smoking, and getting into fights. I walked around with a chip on my shoulder and an "I don't care" attitude.

- **I felt invisible, unimportant, and unworthy.** Deep down, I only wanted to be accepted as I was. I wanted to belong. I wanted to be loved.

I ought my wishes were answered when I was sixteen.
I m t a man five years older than me. He showered his
love nd affection on me and made me feel as if I was the
mos mportant person on earth. Six months later, I was a
high school dropout, pregnant teen living on public
assis nce. I felt more alienated than ever before.
Ever where I went, I felt judged and looked down upon. I
felt espair and was certain my life was over. I had no
futu . I knew I was destined to live a miserable life.

I felt truly alone in the world.

Except I wasn't alone; I had a baby growing inside me. The day I gave birth to my son and saw his angelic face, I knew that it was up to me to break this cycle of self-destructive thoughts and actions.

That's when everything changed!

I began to read every self-help book I could get my hands on. I was on a mission of self-discovery and self-love. I began to let go of the old beliefs that prevented me from seeing myself as capable, intelligent, and beautiful.

The more I let go of those old beliefs, the more confident I became, the more I accomplished. It was a powerful lesson in how changing my thoughts resulted in changing my life.

Six years later, at twenty-three, I earned my master's degree in nursing and became a Nurse Practitioner. Since then, I have dedicated over eighteen years of my life working in adolescent health. I love using my gift and passion to empower teens to create a bright future for themselves.

As I reflect on my painful teen years, I realize how I played a major role in determining my life experiences. My low confidence had paralyzed me from taking action, thus reinforcing my misguided belief that I was different or inferior.

I knew I had to share this knowledge to help teens avoid some of the pain I had experienced.

In my twenty-plus year career specializing in Adolescent Health, I have:

- Established, owned, and operated Teen Confidence Academy, specializing in helping teens overcome stress, anxiety, and depressive symptoms without medication or long-term traditional therapy,
- Established, owned, and operated multiple "Teen Choice Medical Center" locations,
- Become a Speaker, Podcaster and Multi-Award-Winning Author,
- Educated and supported thousands of teens and adults to overcome stress, anxiety, and depressive symptoms,
- Raised a loving, intelligent, and confident man (he is my pride and joy), and
- Completed post-graduate training in holistic and alternative health and healing methods.

I m deeply passionate about helping teens let go of thei barriers to see the beauty and greatness within then elves. I believe each of us deserves a life full of heal , love, and happiness. I also believe that every person has ithin them all the resources needed to achieve a beau ful and fulfilling life.

V en I was going through my troubled teen years, I neec 1 a place where I could be mentored, where I could lear reflect, and grow; a place where I could heal and get a p per, healthy perspective of myself and the world arou 1 me. I didn't have that option then, or at least I didn't kno where to find it.

T t is why I became a Mindset Mentor specializing in teen onfidence, and that's why I am writing this book for you w.

Thousands of teens are living in quiet desperation right now because no one has shown them the key to their success. My goal in writing this book is to teach you about your mind so you can control your thoughts, feelings, and actions. You can take charge of creating the life that you want and deserve.

You deserve to be successful and happy in life. Let's make it happen!

Jacqui Letran

Acknowledgements

I wo d like to express a heartfelt thank you to my best friend and isband, Joseph Wolfgram. Without his love, endless hour of revisions, and support, this book would not have been oossible. Thank you for patiently listening to me talk abot this book endlessly.

T my son, Alan Letran, thank you for being my biggest life t icher and a source of endless love.

T my family, thank you for believing in me and cheering me (It means so much to me to have your love and support.

T my editor, Coral Coons, thank you so much for your prof sionalism and expert advice. You are a joy to work with

T all of my clients, teachers, and mentors, whether in a prof sional relationship or in life experiences, a big thank you r being a part of my life. Your presence in my life has help me grow and transform from a scared little girl into a conf ent, healthy, and happy woman.

L t, but not least, I like to express my gratitude to my ama ng Beta Readers: Ingrid Abild-Pedersen, Candice Betty, Jacq line Corley, Ricci DePass, Sally Guyatt, Theresa Hart an, Cristy Mosher, Joan Norton, Kaye A. Peters, Chri na Raines, Mercedes Silver, and Lesa Smith. I truly appr iate you. Your feedback is invaluable and has made this bool ven more applicable and enjoyable for readers.

Connect with Me

I love hearing from my readers.
Please feel free to connect with me at:

Amazon.com/Author/JacquiLetran

www.JacquiLetran.com

Facebook.com/JacquiLetran

Linkedin.com/in/JacquiLetran

Instagram.com/JacquiLetran

You can also contact me at:
Author@JacquiLetran.com

Thank you so much for reading.
If you enjoyed this book, please consider leaving an honest
review with your favorite online store. It would help other
readers discover this book as well.

Thank you in advance!
Jacqui

Words of Wisdom for Teens Series
Award-Winning Guides for Teen Girls

5 Simple Steps to Manage your Mood
A uide for Teen Girls: How to Let Go of Negative Feelings and Create a Happy Relationship with Yourself and Others

I Would, but MY DAMN MIND Won't Let Me
Guide for Teen Girls: How to Understand and Control Your Thoughts and Feelings

J 1p-Start Your Confidence and Boost Your Self-Esteem
A G de for Teen Girls: Unleash Your Inner Superpowers to Destroy Fear and Self-Doubt, and Build Unshakable Confidence

Companion Journals

5 Simple Steps to Manage your Mood Journal
A 'ompanion Journal to Help You Track, Understand and Take Charge of Your Mood

I Would, but MY DAMN MIND Won't Let Me
A Cc panion Journal to Help You Tap into the Power of Your Mind to Be Positive, Happy, and Confident.

Pre-order now on Amazon

1mp-Start Your Confidence and Boost Your Self-Esteem
A (mpanion Journal to Help You Create a Positive and Powerful Mindset to Conquer Anxiety, Fear, and Self-Doubt

Pre-order now on Amazon

Stop the Bully Within Podcast

After seeing thousands of clients, I noticed a common theme among most of those I help—they are their own biggest bully.

Just pause for a moment and think of the words you say to yourself when you did something wrong or failed at something. Are those loving and supportive words? Would you say those same words to someone you love?

For many people, when they think of a bully, they think of someone outside of them—someone who says and does mean things to cause others pain. Not too many people think about the bully they have within themselves.

I'm on a mission to bring awareness to how damaging this "bully within" can be, and to help people learn how to transform that inner critic into their best friend, cheerleader, and personal champion for success.

Listen to the Podcast at:
https://www.JacquiLetran.com/podcast

Made in the USA
Columbia, SC
26 May 2024

36203431R00076